NEW CRAFTS

BEADWORK

NEW CRAFTS
BEADWORK

ISABEL STANLEY

PHOTOGRAPHY BY PETER WILLIAMS

LORENZ BOOKS

This edition first published in 1997
by Lorenz Books, 27 West 20th Street,
New York, NY 10011

Lorenz Books are available for bulk
purchase for sales promotion and for
premium use. For details, write or call
the manager of special sales,
Lorenz Books, 27 West 20th Street,
New York, NY 10011
(800) 354-9657

Lorenz Books is an imprint of
Anness Publishing Limited

ISBN 1 85967 531 X

Publisher: Joanna Lorenz
Senior Editor: Lindsay Porter
Designer: Lilian Lindblom
Photographer: Peter Williams
Stylist: Georgina Rhodes
Illustrators: Madeleine David
and Vana Haggerty

Printed in Hong Kong / China

10 9 8 7 6 5 4 3 2

CONTENTS

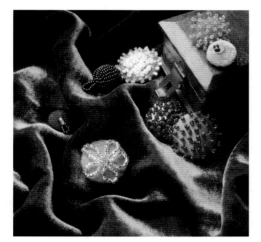

INTRODUCTION

B EADS ARE SIMPLE DECORATIVE OBJECTS, USUALLY ROUND, WITH A HOLE THROUGH THE CENTER. THEY MAY BE ANY SHAPE AND SIZE AND CAN BE MADE FROM A VARIETY OF MATERIALS. BEADS APPEAL TO BOTH THE EYE AND THE TOUCH. THEY CAN SPARKLE AND SHIMMER AND ADD WEIGHT, RICHNESS AND DEPTH TO ANY CRAFT WORK. THE FIRST "BEADS" WERE NATURAL FINDS SUCH AS COWRIE SHELLS, FEATHERS, SEEDS, BONES AND WOOD. ALTHOUGH OUR ANCESTORS ADMIRED THESE TRIMMINGS FOR THEIR AESTHETIC QUALITIES, THEY ALSO REGARDED THEM AS TALISMANS IMBUED WITH MYSTICAL POWER. THEY BELIEVED THAT STRINGS OF BEADS COULD PROTECT THE WEARER FROM HARMFUL INFLUENCES AND BRING GOOD FORTUNE. BEADS WERE APPLIED ON THE EDGES OF CLOTHES AND COVERINGS TO ENHANCE THEIR PROTECTIVE QUALITIES. SHINY REFLECTIVE MATERIALS, SUCH AS MICA, SILVER OR BRASS, WERE THOUGHT TO DEFLECT THE EVIL EYE. AS SOCIETIES GREW MORE SOPHISTICATED, NEW MATERIALS AND TECHNIQUES WERE EMPLOYED AND THE ART OF COMMERCIAL BEAD MAKING DEVELOPED.

Left: Beads bring color and light to almost any object. They can be made from wood, metal, plastic — or even semiprecious stones.

HISTORY OF BEADWORK

Historically, the role of beads in society has not been merely simple ornamentation; beads have had great cultural significance. Some historians view beads as important artifacts that reflect economic, religious and social conditions. Beads and beadwork are constantly changing and evolving, influenced both by fashion and by technological advancements.

During the fifteenth century, beads became an important trading currency. European explorers used them as gifts to the indigenous peoples of North America to initiate friendship and trust. As trade grew between the Native Americans and European merchants, beads and steel needles were exchanged mainly for skins. The imported glass beads soon replaced locally made bone and shell beads, which had been applied to hides with moose hair and porcupine quills. The Native Americans adopted the fluid floral styles of the foreigners and assimilated them with their own traditional patterns to make beautiful and distinctive moccasins, pipe bags and skirts.

Commercially manufactured beads were first introduced to Africa in the fifteenth century by Asians and Europeans. Caravan routes carried the easily portable currency deep into the continent. Merchants traded their glass beads for ivory, skins and even slaves. The more valuable and rare beads quickly became prized possessions, indicators of the wealth and status of the wearer. Such was the social significance of certain beads that only upper strata of society were allowed to wear them. The etiquette of beads highlighted other differences apart from social hierarchy. Particular combinations and patterns, as well as the exact position of a given piece, identified the married and the unmarried, or the young and the old. Furthermore, these differences reflected the personal achievements and the birthplace or village of an individual. Certain elaborately beaded

costumes took on special significance and could be worn only by participants during ceremonial performances, weddings and initiation rites.

The Zulu people and the Ndbele-speaking people are particularly well known for their bead craftsmanship. Men and women wore necklaces, headbands, belts, bangles and anklets that were made from narrow lengths of bead weaving and beaded, wrapped rope and worn with skins and fur. Women of different status

Above: A highly decorated Native American beaded cloth sash, together with beaded moccasins and bag. European traders first brought precious glass beads, known as "trade beads" or "pony beads," to the American continent, where they were used as a form of currency. Their trading partners took to them with enthusiasm and integrated them into their existing artistic traditions. Before long, beadwork became an integral part of costume in the entire region.

were distinguished by heavily beaded girdles, aprons, coats and hats. Young women sent color- and pattern-coded messages in beadwork to their lovers when they were far from home.

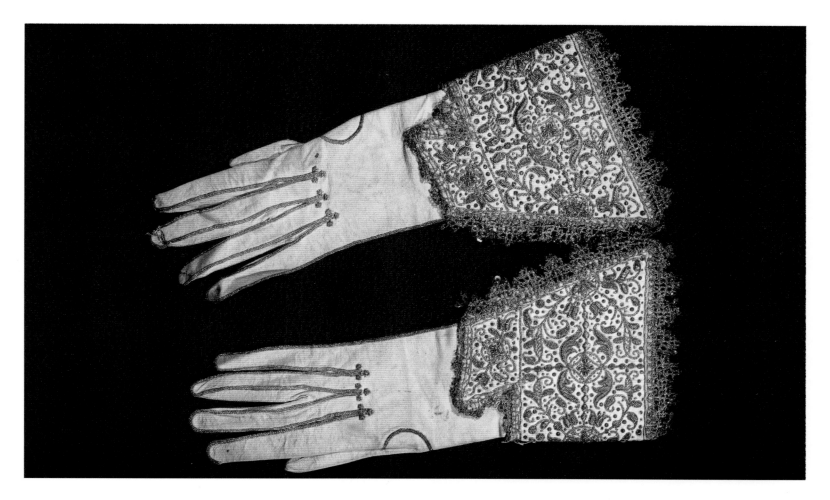

In medieval England, the wearing of beads and embroidery had a ceremonial function. The first manufactured beads were made from expensive raw materials such as precious and semiprecious stones. They were available only to the nobility and the clergy. Professional embroiderers embellished rich fabrics during the first great period of excellence in English embroidery, the "Opus Anglicum." Drilled pearls and coral were applied with metallic threads to make elaborate and heavy ecclesiastical vestments. These garments must have been a wondrous sight as they sparkled and gleamed in the candlelit churches. The beads used were so valuable that, when the importance of the church declined, the prized beads were removed and recycled. In the early years of the sixteenth century, some of these stones were then embroidered onto the extravagant costumes of the Tudor nobility. This ushered in a second period of superior craftsmanship. Traveling needlewomen created fabulously rich costumes that were stiff with embroidery and heavy with pearls, spangles, sequins and corals. These gloriously impractical costumes both indicated the importance of the wearer and rendered him or her virtually helpless, unable to dress or undress without a coterie of servants.

In the middle of the seventeenth century, young ladies were encouraged to

Above: Gloves of white kid embroidered in silver thread and sequins, from the mid-seventeenth century. Such luxury items were a potent sign of status, indicators of both wealth and leisure.

practice and display their needle- and beadworking skills by producing textile jewel boxes as part of their "education." They used a technique now known as stump work, in which three-dimensional or padded embroidery is worked with silk thread and wool yarn and embellished with small glass beads, spangles and mica. These wonderful caskets feature houses, their elaborately dressed inhabitants and landscaped gardens, a particular seventeenth-century preoccupation. The gardens

were crammed with exotic flowers, plants and trees, sometimes three-dimensional, and worked with beads threaded onto wire and bent into shape. The bizarre proportions of the features indicate that they were not observed, but copied from illustrations.

During the nineteenth century, embroidery and beadwork became popular hobbies among upper- and middle-class ladies. These gentle pursuits were employment enough for privileged women who did not have to work, and the results demonstrated not only the status of the women but also the qualities of femininity, patience and diligence that were then considered desirable.

Victorian ladies also made delicate three-dimensional pieces, such as butterflies, flowers and insects, by threading beads onto wire. They arranged the finished structures as displays under glass domes or used them to make corsages, tiaras and combs for themselves and as gifts for friends and family.

A passion emerged for using scraps of rich fabrics recycled from favorite dresses to make abstract patchworks. These patchwork quilts were scattered liberally with embroidery stitches, ribbons, buttons, glass beads and sequins.

Beadwork was not just the preserve of women, however – sailors at sea labored over tokens of affection for their loved ones at home. They made patchwork pin-cushions using scraps of wool fabric from uniforms and stuffed with sawdust, and spelled out sentimental messages of love and remembrance in beads and sequins threaded onto pins and pressed firmly into the cushion.

The most important craft, however, was Berlinwork, or canvas covered with

Left: Two Victorian Berlinwork vests.

Left: The charts, samplers and slipper tops pictured here were all made in Europe and date from 1840 to 1860. All are examples of Berlinwork, the most popular form of Victorian beaded embroidery.

Below: This diaphanous painted silk voile evening dress was first worn in Paris in 1922; its delicate beadwork creates a stunning shimmering effect, in the low-waisted, showstopping fashion of the time. Although it is quite ornate, a garment such as this was far easier to wear than the boned, corseted gowns of previous decades. The long beaded necklace is a classic accessory of the Roaring Twenties.

tent or cross-stitch worked in wool yarn. This craze swept across Europe and America, its popularity based on the ease with which it could be worked. To take advantage of such a huge market, manufacturers produced thousands of patterns and different-colored threads and yarns. Some patterns featured bead-work. Tiny brass, or more often glass, beads were stitched in place of yarn to give a shim-mery surface to the piece. Different tones were used to give a mottled effect, known as "grisaille work." Homes were filled with bags, tea cosies, covers, bedspreads, slippers, cushions and fire screens, the results of the labors of women.

Throughout the latter half of the nine-teenth century there was a craze for evening dresses with bodices heavily beaded with jet and small glass beads, and for small bags embellished with fringes and tassels.

During the 1920s, women's lives changed rapidly as they celebrated the end of the Great War, voted for the first time and began to enter the workplace. Fashions reflected this freedom. Narrow

low-waisted dresses dripped with rows of fringes of sequins, bugle, drop and glass beads. The shorter styles of dress allowed greater freedom of movement, and the swinging fringes were designed to dazzle while the wearers danced the new jazz-age dances. The popularity of beadwork declined with the onset of the Second World War, as rationing meant that clothes became simpler and more austere. In recent years, however, beaded fashions and crafts have had a revival.

Today, beads are produced in great numbers and variety. The incredible choice of beads on the market allows contemporary designers and craft artists to explore the intrinsic beauty and cre-ative possibilities of beads.

GALLERY

BEADWORK IS A CENTURIES-OLD CRAFT WITH A RICH HISTORY. TODAY, DESIGNERS AND CRAFTSPEOPLE ARE DRAWN TO THE MEDIUM FOR ITS DECORATIVE QUALITIES AND VERSATILITY. ONCE MORE, BEADS ARE AS LIKELY TO BE FOUND IN HAUTE COUTURE AS IN A CRAFT STORE. BEADWORK CAN BE MADE IN A WIDE VARIETY OF STYLES, FROM THE REASSURINGLY TRADITIONAL TO THE UNEXPECTEDLY MODERN, AS THESE EXAMPLES OF CONTEMPORARY WORK SHOW.

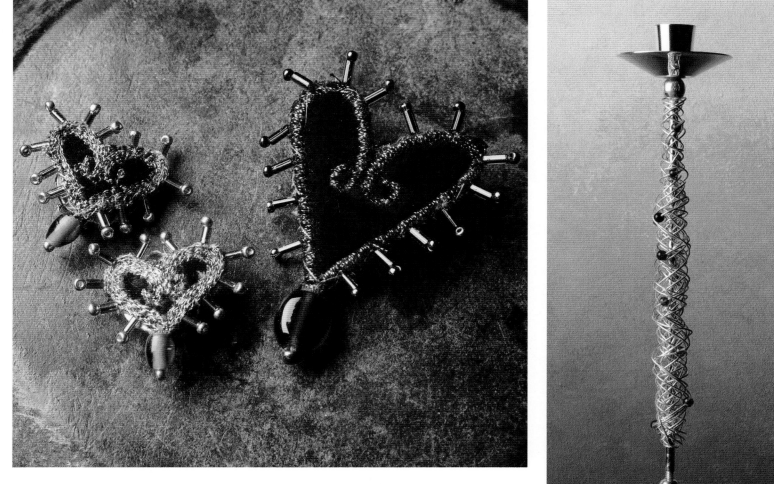

Above: BROOCH AND EARRINGS
The heart-shaped brooch and matching earrings are made from rich velvet fabric worked with gold machine embroidery and finished with decorative beaded fringing.
ISABEL STANLEY

Right: CANDLESTICK
This elegant candlestick has a metal base and is embellished with beads strung on wire and wrapped along the shaft.
LIBERTY

Above left: BEADED
FLOWERS
These decorative beaded
flowers are made from
crystal chips, garnets and a
variety of small and bugle
beads, by working out
from the center of the
flower and building up the
petals. They can be pinned
or sewn onto garments or
headgear as trims. Draw
inspiration from fresh
flowers or books.
JANICE MARR

Above right: PEARLIZED
SEQUINS
If circumstances do not
allow you to dress from
head to toe in sequins
and pearls, then console
yourself by adding
strategic detail with strips
of pearlized sequins. A
bead loom is used to
create a woven strip
studded at intervals with
fake pearls for a taste of
delicious luxury.
KAREN SPURGIN

Right: BEADED
CANDLE JAR
Small red beads glow like
jewels and let the warm
candlelight show through
the wire structure of this
beaded candle jar. In any
project that exposes beads
to heat, care should be
taken to use materials that
are neither hazardous nor
likely to melt in the heat
of a flame.
LIBERTY

Opposite: BEADED FRUIT
Scraps of duchess satin and antique velvet have been beaded with cup sequins, small beads and crystal chips. For tactile appeal they have been filled with lentils, like little bean bags. The stems are made of twisted jewelry wire and beads, some shaped like leaves.
KAREN SPURGIN

Right: BEADED BUSTIER
This stunning piece was worked on a wire base with beads woven in and out of the basic shape.
DIANA LAURIE

Below left: SILVER SUNGLASS FRAMES
Beads are woven in and out of a wire frame for these glamorous glasses. Old necklaces found at flea-market stalls are a good source of beads with distinctive character.
DIANA LAURIE

Below right:
DECORATIVE DISKS
Details such as these decorative disks turn a basic fabric into something for a special occasion.
KAREN SPURGIN

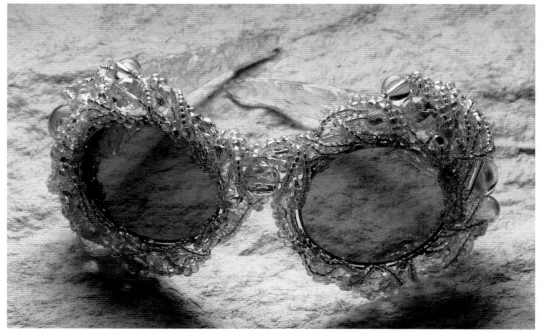

BEADS

MANY CRAFT SHOPS AND MAIL-ORDER SUPPLIERS NOW SPECIALIZE IN BEADS. THERE IS AN ENORMOUS RANGE OF STYLES, SHAPES AND TEXTURES TO CHOOSE FROM—GLASS, METAL, WOOD, MOTHER-OF-PEARL, SEMIPRECIOUS STONES AND MODERN SYNTHETIC IMITATIONS.

Bugle beads Narrow glass tubes widely available in many sizes, these are particularly effective used in contrast with small glass beads.

Crystals Usually cut glass, these beads have a faceted surface and are available in different shapes, such as hearts and diamonds. Use beeswax to protect the beading thread from their sharp edges.

Drop beads Shaped like teardrops, these are normally used to finish a strand or area of work.

Found objects Many objects, such as bottle caps, coins and driftwood, make interesting beads. Use a fine drill to make a hole through the center. Always use protective eyewear when drilling glass beads.

Lampwork beads Made in India, these glass beads are decorated with molten glass trailed in patterns such as leaves or flowers. Some lampwork beads have an insert of silver foil.

Metal beads These beads, often in complex shapes in brass or copper, may be silver- or gold-plated. They are most often used in jewelry to separate larger beads or at the end of a string.

Millefiori Long poles of colored glass are fused together, then sliced into mosaiclike cross sections, literally "thousand flowers." These beads are now also available in plastic.

Natural materials Beads made from nuts, seeds, shells, mother-of-pearl and bone are regarded as potent talismans in some countries. Soft wooden beads are more suited to jewelry than embroidery.

Pearl beads Artificial pearl beads with a pearlized finish are available in colors as well as white and ivory.

Pottery beads Clay beads were originally made by inserting a wooden stick through the clay shapes. During firing, the stick burned away to leave a hole. The blue-and-white porcelain beads shown at right are of traditional Chinese design.

Rocailles These small, slightly flattened glass beads are very popular. Many varieties, such as opaque, transparent, metallic and iridescent, are available. Sometimes the hole is lined with iridescent or opaque color, gold or silver.

Semiprecious stones Stones such as amber, turquoise, coral and jade are expensive, but imitations are also available.

Sequins Flat plastic shapes such as stars, flowers and leaves, with one or two holes, are available in different colors and finishes. Originally sequins were made from sheets of gold and silver.

Small glass beads Small glass beads, also known as seeds, are used in many beading projects. They are spherical but, like flatter rocailles, they come in many varieties. They are sometimes sold prestrung, ready to transfer to a needle.

Venetian glass beads These highly decorative beads are from one of the world's most famous bead-making centers.

Wound beads Molten glass is wound around a rotating metal rod to create swirling striped patterns.

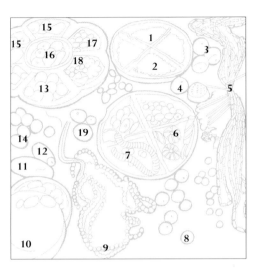

1 Rocailles	11 Lampwork beads
2 Small glass beads	12 Wound bead
3 Venetian beads	13 Artificial pearls
4 Millefiori	14 Crystals
5 Bugle beads	15 Semiprecious stones
6 Bone beads	– lapis lazuli, etc.
7 Sequins	16 Pottery beads
8 Drop beads	17 Wooden beads
9 Prestrung beads	18 Metal beads
10 Found objects	19 Amber

MATERIALS

ONLY A FEW BASIC MATERIALS ARE NEEDED IN BEADWORK, DEPENDING ON THE PROJECT. THE MAIN MATERIALS USED ARE, OF COURSE, THE BEADS THEMSELVES. YOU MAY ALREADY HAVE MANY OF THE OTHER MATERIALS IN YOUR SEWING BASKET. MANY ITEMS ARE AVAILABLE AT NOTIONS DEPARTMENTS OR FROM MAIL-ORDER SUPPLIERS. FOR FURTHER DETAILS, SEE THE SUPPLIER INFORMATION AT THE BACK OF THE BOOK.

Beading thread This is a special thread designed for beadwork. A strong, smooth thread such as polyester is equally effective.

Beading wire This is available in gold, copper and silver, and in many diameter sizes; 0.4 mm and 0.6 mm are the most useful. Check that the wire will fit through the hole in the bead.

Bookbinding fabric This closely woven cotton fabric has a paper backing that can be glued. It is available at specialty bookbinding suppliers.

Brass screw binders Available at specialty bookbinding suppliers, these are used to hold sheaves of paper together to make a book.

Buttons Mix buttons with beads for extra decorative effect.

Cord Beads can be wrapped around a core of three-ply cord, available in many colors at furniture-trimmings suppliers and notions departments.

Cotton spheres These are made of compressed cotton fibers and come in various shapes. They are available at specialty trimmings and beading suppliers.

Cover buttons Sold in kit form at notions departments, cover buttons consist of two pieces: a top, over which the fabric is pulled, and an underside with shank attached.

Embroidery threads These include perlé cotton (a high-sheen two-ply thread), stranded embroidery floss (separate the six-ply strands for fine work) and machine embroidery threads. They are available in a full range of colors, including metallics.

Fabric paints Water-based, nontoxic paints that are set by ironing are recommended.

Fishing twine For heavy beads, such as glass, fishing twine is recommended. It is stronger than polyester thread but more difficult to work with.

Floss thread This fibrous thread has a silklike sheen.

Fusible bonding web Ironed onto the back of appliqué fabric, this bonds it to the ground fabric stitching.

Interfacing Normally used to stiffen fabric, it also makes a good ground fabric for beadwork.

Jewelry findings Gold- or silver-plated hatpins, earring wires, clasps, brooch backs and other findings are available at beadwork suppliers.

Marker This is useful for marking outlines and is also used for drawing decorative patterns.

Ribbon Silk, satin and velvet ribbons can all be used to embellish beadwork.

Sequin pins Shorter than dressmaker's pins, these are ideal for pin beading.

Tape Fringes are stitched to fabric tape before being inserted into seams or rolled into tassels.

Tapestry canvas This stiff, open-weave canvas is available in various sizes of weave at embroidery suppliers.

Tapestry yarn This matte wool yarn comes in a wide range of colors.

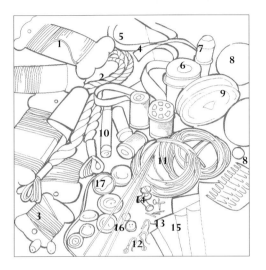

1 Tapestry yarn	10 Floss thread
2 Cord	11 Beading wire
3 Beading thread	12 Jewelry findings
4 Tape	13 Sequin pins
5 Ribbon	14 Brass screw binders
6 Fabric paint	15 Bookbinding fabric
7 Fabric paint	16 Buttons
8 Cotton spheres	17 Cover buttons
9 Fishing twine	

EQUIPMENT

BEADWORK IS AN IDEAL SMALL-SCALE HOBBY, AS IT REQUIRES VERY FEW SPECIALTY TOOLS. BASIC EQUIPMENT SUCH AS SCISSORS, PINS AND A RULER WILL PROBABLY BE ALREADY CLOSE AT HAND IN A SEWING BASKET OR AROUND THE HOUSE. STORE YOUR BEADS IN SEPARATE GLASS OR PLASTIC CONTAINERS, WHERE YOU CAN FIND THEM QUICKLY. WHEN YOU ARE WORKING ON A PROJECT, DECANT THEM INTO SMALL WHITE PALETTES OR SHALLOW SAUCERS.

Bead loom This small loom is specially designed for beadwork. The warp threads are fitted between metal springs and wound around wooden rollers. Bead looms are available at many craft stores.

Beading needles These fine, long needles are available in various sizes and can be used to thread several beads at a time. They break easily, so they require careful handling. To thread beads with large holes, you can also use "between" needles.

Beeswax This is used to run along the beading thread to increase its strength and prevent it from snagging on sharp edges. It is particularly useful when threading faceted beads.

Craft knife A strong knife is needed to cut out cardboard.

Drawing pins These are used to pin strands onto a pin board.

Dressmaker's pins These are used to pin fabric before basting or slip stitching.

Embroidery hoop Two tightly fitting rings hold fabric taut. Plastic hoops with a metal spring are recommended for use under a sewing machine.

Embroidery scissors These small, sharp scissors are used to cut and trim thread and fabric.

Fabric marker The marks made with this specialized pen fade on contact with air or water.

Graph paper This is used to measure fringes and tassels.

Metal scissors Use metal scissors to crack damaged beads and thus remove them from a string.

Needles Some dressmaking needles, called "sharps," may be small enough to pass through beads. Leather needles are used to stitch beads to tough material such as leather.

Paintbrush This is used to apply fabric paint in some projects.

Palettes When working on a project, decant beads into white china palettes, available at art-supply stores. Alternatively, you can use saucers, as long as you do not mix up the different types of beads.

Pin board Fringing or macramé work should be pinned out on a board. It is important that the board is large enough to accommodate the whole design. Small pieces of work can be pinned out on an ironing board.

Ruler This is essential for accurate measuring. A metal-edged ruler is the most suitable for these projects.

Sewing machine Use the normal foot for straight stitching and the darning foot for machine embroidery.

Tape measure Use instead of a ruler for measuring fabric and curved surfaces.

Tweezers These are very useful for both selecting and removing individual beads.

Wire cutters and round-nosed jewelry pliers These are essential for bending and cutting wire.

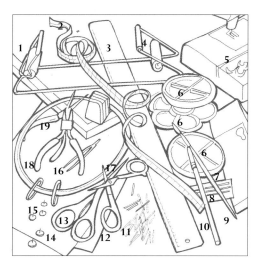

1 Pin board	11 Pins
2 Tape measure	12 Embroidery scissors
3 Ruler	13 Metal scissors
4 Bead loom	14 Graph paper
5 Sewing machine	15 Drawing pins
6 Palettes	16 Tweezers
7 Needles	17 Embroidery hoop
8 Beading needles	18 Wire cutters
9 Paintbrush	19 Round-nosed
10 Fabric marker	jewelry pliers

BASIC TECHNIQUES

THE TECHNIQUES USED IN BEADWORK ARE QUITE EASY TO GRASP ONCE YOU UNDERSTAND THE FUNDAMENTAL PRINCIPLES. HOWEVER, WHEN LEARNING ANY NEW SKILL, IT IS WORTH TAKING TIME TO MASTER THE BASICS BEFORE PROGRESSING TO MORE ADVANCED TECHNIQUES. START WITH A STRAIGHTFORWARD PROJECT SUCH AS STRINGING BEADS OR MAKING A SHORT FRINGE, THEN PROGRESS TO MORE INTRICATE WORK.

PRESTRUNG BEADS

Simply thread a needle and pass it through the beads, then remove the old thread.

BEAD PICOT

Use a tape measure and fabric marker to mark even points. Thread a needle, insert it into the fabric at one end of the picot and secure with a knot. Pass the needle through a large bead, followed by a small bead – the small bead will prevent the large one from slipping off. Push both beads as far as possible up the needle, then pass the needle back through the large bead. Make a stitch in the fabric to the next marked point.

LONG FRINGE

1 For an even fringe, use graph paper or count the number of beads and use the same number for each string. Cut a piece of thread four times the length of the fringe desired. Thread both ends through a needle to give a doubled thread. Insert into fabric and secure with a knot. Pass needle through loop in thread and pull taut.

2 Mark the length of the fringe on graph paper and place next to the thread. Thread on the required number of beads, pushing them up as far as possible.

3 Pass the needle through the second-to-last bead. Check that no thread is visible. Make a fastening-off stitch between the third and fourth beads from the end, then continue up the string of beads, making fastening-off stitches every four beads.

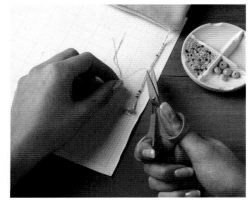

4 Pull the string gently to remove kinks in the thread, then trim the thread.

SHORT FRINGE

This is worked with a continuous length of thread. Mark the length desired on graph paper. Insert the needle in the fabric and secure the thread with a knot. Thread on the required number of beads, pushing them up as far as possible. Pass the needle through the second-to-last bead, then back up the full length of the string. Insert the needle back into the fabric and bring it out at the next point on the fringe.

POINTED FRINGE

Thread a needle, insert in the fabric and secure with a knot. Thread on a bugle bead, a small glass bead and another bugle. Push the beads up as far as possible to form points, then insert the needle at the next point on the fringe.

DROP FRINGE

Thread a needle, insert in the fabric and secure with a knot. Thread on a small glass bead, a drop bead and another small glass bead. Push the beads up as far as possible, then insert the needle at the next point on the fringe.

LOOPS

Mark points at even intervals with a fabric marker. Thread a needle, insert into the fabric at the first point and secure with a knot. Thread on enough beads to give the desired size loop, pushing them up as far as possible. Insert the needle back at the same point to form a loop, then insert the needle at the next point on the fringe.

LOOPS WITH STEMS

Before making a loop, thread on the required number of beads for the stem, then add the beads for the loop. Pass the needle back through the stem.

NEEDLE-WOVEN BEADING

In this technique, a continuous thread runs through rounds of beads, with the second round of beads fitting between pairs of the first. The second round is joined to the first by interweaving. The following instructions are for a three-dimensional object. For a two-dimensional design, work rows instead of rounds.

1 For round 1, thread on the required number of beads, tie around the neck of the object and knot the ends.

2 For round 2, pass needle through first bead of round 1, then thread first bead of round 2 between first and second beads. Pass needle through third bead of round 1. Continue until design is complete.

COUCHING

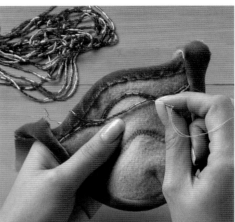

Prestrung beads are laid down on fabric to create or embellish the lines of the design, then stitched over (couched down) with thread to secure. Add a second thread of beads on top for extra texture.

SCALLOPS

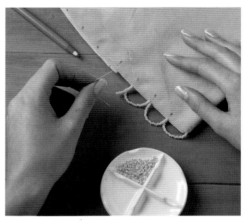

Mark points at even intervals. Thread a needle, insert it into the fabric at the first point and secure with a knot. Thread on enough beads to give the desired-length scallop, pushing them up as far as possible, then insert the needle back in at the next point.

THREADING A BEAD LOOM

Bead weaving produces flat, narrow strips of beaded fabric. The beads lie between the warp threads, and a continuous weft thread is passed through the beads, over and under the warp threads.

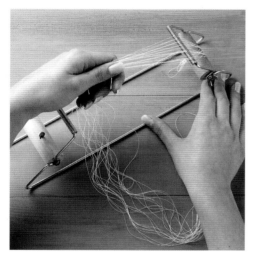

1 Decide the length of the piece required and add 18 inches. Cut the warp threads to this length. Calculate the number of beads required for the width, depending on the size of bead.
Cut one warp thread for each bead, plus one extra. Lay the warp threads out smoothly and tie them together with a knot at each end. Divide the strands evenly in half, then slip one knot over the rivets in the roller. Turn the roller to wind on a little thread, then spread the threads out and arrange them in the spring next to each other.

2 Slip the knot at the other end of the warp over the rivets in the other roller and wind on as before. Adjust the tension by winding the rollers until the warp threads are taut.

3 Thread a beading needle with a long length of thread and draw it through beeswax. Tie the other end of the thread to the far left warp thread 1 inch from the rollers.

CHINESE NECKLACE

THE STARTING POINT FOR THIS NECKLACE WAS THE UNUSUAL FILIGREE PENDANT AT THE CENTER. THE BEADS ARE STRUNG ON A KNOTTED LENGTH. BLANKET STITCH IS WORKED AROUND A CORE OF THREAD, THE STITCHES SPIRALING AROUND THE THREAD NATURALLY.

1 For each side cut two-ply silk thread 40 inches long, fold in half and pin midpoint to pin board. Cut two lengths of fine silk 80 inches long. Thread each onto a large-eyed needle, double up thread, tie a knot and slip both knots over pin. Lay fine silk thread next to the two-ply lengths. Work a blanket stitch along the threads for 4¾ inches.

2 Separate the two-ply strands and, using the two needles, work a blanket stitch for 1 inch down both lengths.

3 Thread one bone bead onto one strand, and one round amber bead onto the other. Tie double knots just beneath the beads. Continue as for step 1 for another ½ inch.

4 Thread a round lampwork and tie a knot just beneath the bead. Continue as one strand for ½ inch, divide in two for ½ inch, thread on two precious stone beads, and tie knots.

5 Continue as two strands for ½ inch, then attach the strands. Continue as one strand for ½ inch, thread on lampwork disk, knot and continue as one strand for ½ inch. Thread on first one bone, then one large amber and another bone bead. Tie a knot.

6 Tie two sides together, thread all ends through pendant and knot. Thread ends through a lampwork disk and knot. Thread end back through oval bead and trim. Unpin piece and sew clasp to each end.

MATERIALS AND EQUIPMENT YOU WILL NEED

TWO-PLY SILK THREAD • SCISSORS • MEASURING TAPE • DRAWING PINS • PIN BOARD • FINE SILK THREAD • TWO LARGE-EYED NEEDLES •
SIX BONE BEADS • TWO ROUND AMBER BEADS • TWO ROUND LAMPWORK BEADS WITH FOIL INSERTS • FOUR PRECIOUS STONE BEADS • THREE LAMP-
WORK DISKS WITH FOIL INSERTS • TWO LARGE AMBER BEADS • ONE LARGE CHINESE PENDANT • ONE CLASP

VENETIAN NECKLACE

IN THIS SUMPTUOUS CREATION, MULTIPLE STRANDS OF RICHLY COLORED BEADS ARE JOINED AT INTERVALS WITH LARGE VENETIAN BEADS. THIS IS AN IDEAL WAY TO SHOW OFF A FEW PRECIOUS BEADS BY MIXING THEM WITH A SELECTION OF SMALL INEXPENSIVE BEADS IN CONTRASTING COLORS. CRIMPING BEADS ARE DESIGNED SO THAT THEY CAN BE FIRMLY ATTACHED WITH PLIERS TO SAFELY HOLD THE FASTENINGS FOR A HEAVY NECKLACE.

1 Cut 100 inches of thread and thread through a needle. Tie a bead to the end as an anchor. Thread on the following beads: one lilac, 25 bronze, one green, two bronze, two green, one red, three green, one red, one lilac, one Venetian, one lilac, one red, three green, one red, two green, two bronze, one green. Repeat this sequence six more times. End with 25 bronze and a lilac.

2 Cut another 100-inch length of thread, thread through the needle and tie around the anchor bead as before. Pass the needle through the first lilac bead threaded in step 1, then thread on 25 bronze, one green, two bronze, two green, one red and three green. Pass the needle through the red, lilac, Venetian, lilac and red beads threaded in step 1. Repeat this sequence six more times, ending with 25 bronze beads and passing the needle through the lilac bead.

3 Make another three strands the same way. Tie the threads in a tight knot at each end, then attach a brass crimping bead over each knot with pliers.

4 Attach a gold loop to the top of each crimping bead. Thread the fastener through the loops.

MATERIALS AND EQUIPMENT YOU WILL NEED

SCISSORS • STRONG BLACK NYLON THREAD • NEEDLE • ¼-INCH LILAC IRIDESCENT AND RED GLASS BEADS •
⅛-INCH BRONZE AND GREEN GLASS BEADS • SEVEN LARGE VENETIAN GLASS BEADS • TWO CRIMPING BEADS WITH LOOPS•
ROUND-NOSED JEWELRY PLIERS • TWO ¼-INCH GOLD LOOPS • ONE S-SHAPED GOLD FASTENER

WRAPPED EARRINGS

THESE RICHLY DECORATIVE EARRINGS ARE SIMPLY MADE OF ROLLED TUBES OF CARDBOARD COVERED WITH VELVET RIBBON. THE TUBES ARE THEN WRAPPED WITH METALLIC THREAD AND GOLD WIRE STUDDED WITH SMALL BEADS; LARGER BEADS ARE ATTACHED WITH HATPINS. RIBBONS AND BEADS ARE BOTH AVAILABLE IN A HUGE RANGE OF COLORS, SO IT IS EASY TO EXPERIMENT WITH DIFFERENT COLOR COMBINATIONS TO MATCH A PARTICULAR OUTFIT.

1 Cut two rectangles of cardboard, each 1½ x 2¾ inches. Starting from the short side, roll into narrow tubes ½ inch in diameter.

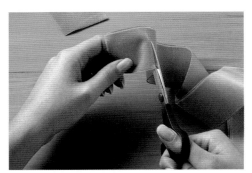

2 Cut two pieces of velvet ribbon, 2½ inches long. Roll a piece of ribbon around each cardboard tube, right side out.

3 Fold under the raw edges of the ribbon and slip-stitch.

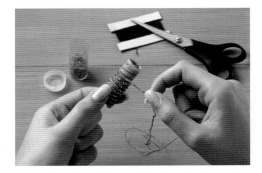

4 Double red metallic thread, thread onto a needle and knot end. Fasten to end of a tube, wrap evenly around tube and tie a knot. Cut 40 pieces of gold wire, ½ inch long. Thread beading thread onto a needle and fasten to a tube. Thread on, alternately, gold wire and green beads. Wrap around the tube and tie a knot.

5 Push a hatpin through the tube ¼ inch from top. Snip ends, leaving an equal length on each side. Thread a flower bead, large red bead and three small red beads on each side. Twist the ends into a spiral.

6 Take a hatpin for each tube, thread on a brass bead, large red bead, hexagonal bead, wrapped tube, and then the same beads in reverse. Trim each hatpin end, then bend into a loop. Attach earring wires.

MATERIALS AND EQUIPMENT YOU WILL NEED

THIN CARDBOARD • RULER AND PENCIL • SCISSORS • 2-INCH-WIDE VELVET RIBBON • SEWING NEEDLE •
SEWING THREAD TO MATCH RIBBON • RED METALLIC EMBROIDERY THREAD • TEXTURED GOLD WIRE • WIRE CUTTERS • BEADING NEEDLE •
MATCHING BEADING THREAD • SMALL GREEN GLASS BEADS • FOUR HATPINS • EIGHT ¼-INCH FLOWER BRASS BEADS •
EIGHT ¼-INCH RED GLASS BEADS • TWELVE ⅛-INCH RED GLASS BEADS • ROUND-NOSED JEWELRY PLIERS •
FOUR ½-INCH HEXAGONAL BRASS BEADS • PAIR OF SILVER EARRING WIRES

BEADED BUTTONS

SIMPLE AND SATISFYING TO MAKE, THESE BEAUTIFUL BUTTONS ADD A UNIQUE FINISHING TOUCH TO A SPECIAL GARMENT OR SOFT FURNISHING PROJECT. THE LUSCIOUS BLACKBERRY BUTTON IS CONSTRUCTED AROUND A COMPRESSED COTTON SPHERE, AND WOULD LOOK EQUALLY ATTRACTIVE AS A PENDANT HANG-ING FROM A BRACELET OR NECKLACE. THE OTHER THREE BUTTONS ARE ALL MADE FROM SCRAPS OF SILK AND TAFFETA, USING COVER BUTTON KITS AS A BASE. CHOOSE BETWEEN THICKLY ENCRUSTED BUTTONS COVERED WITH BEADS AND A SIMPLE TASSEL OR FLOWER DESIGN.

1 For the blackberry button: Using a black marker, cover the cotton sphere completely.

2 Thread the needle and make a few stitches at the top of the sphere to secure. Thread on a small black glass bead, make a stitch, then pass the needle through the sphere. Thread on another bead and stitch down. Take the needle around the sphere, passing through the two beads at top and bottom, then around at right angles to divide it into quarters.

3 Thread on 18 beads and pass the needle through the bottom bead on the sphere. Thread on 18 more beads, pass the needle through the top bead, then wrap it around the sphere at right angles.

MATERIALS AND EQUIPMENT YOU WILL NEED

BLACK MARKER • COMPRESSED COTTON SPHERE, ½ INCH IN DIAMETER • NEEDLE AND BLACK THREAD • SMALL BLACK GLASS BEADS •
FABRIC MARKER • 1¼-INCH-DIAMETER COVER BUTTON • SILK • SCISSORS • THREADS TO MATCH SILK AND TAFFETA•
LARGE TRANSPARENT GLASS BEADS WITH SILVER-LINED HOLES • ¼-INCH GREEN CRYSTAL BEADS • ½-INCH-DIAMETER COVER BUTTONS • TAFFETA •
¼-INCH GREEN GLASS BEAD • SMALL COPPER-COLORED GLASS BEADS • SMALL TRANSPARENT GLASS BEADS

4 Thread on 16 beads and work from top to bottom as before, this time dividing the sphere into eight sections. Repeat with 14 beads, dividing the sphere into 16 sections, until the whole sphere is covered.

6 For the flower button: Using a fabric marker, draw around the 1¼-inch cover button on the silk. Draw another circle ¾ inch larger and cut out. Mark five equally spaced points around the inner circle.

8 Bring the needle out at one of the points marked. Couch down the loop at this point with a stitch between the ninth and tenth beads. Make four more glass-bead petals in the same way.

5 If the blackberry is intended to hang on a bracelet or necklace, fasten a thread at the bottom and thread on eight beads. Insert the needle back into the sphere at the same point to make a loop.

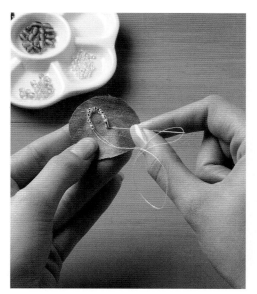

7 Thread a needle and fasten on in the center of the circle. Thread on 20 large transparent glass beads, then insert the needle back at the same point to make a loop.

9 Stitch a green crystal bead in the center of the flower.

▶

10 Run a gathering stitch ⅛ inch from the raw edge. Place the cover button in the center and pull up the thread. Secure with a few small stitches and attach the underside of the button.

11 For the tassel button: Draw around a ½-inch-diameter cover button onto the taffeta, then draw another circle ½ inch larger and cut out. Thread a needle and stick it through the center. Thread on the green glass bead and eight copper beads, then pass the needle back through the green bead and tie a knot. Gather the raw edges and attach the cover button as in step 10.

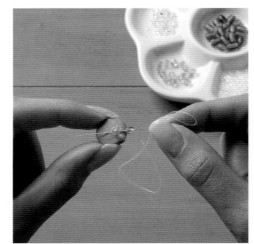

12 For the jewel-encrusted button: Draw around the cover button on the taffeta, then draw another circle ¼ inch larger and cut out. Run a gathering stitch around the edge and attach the cover button as in step 10. Thread a needle and stick it through the center. Thread on a green crystal bead and some small transparent glass beads, then pass the needle back through the green bead. Make another stitch and repeat until the button is completely covered.

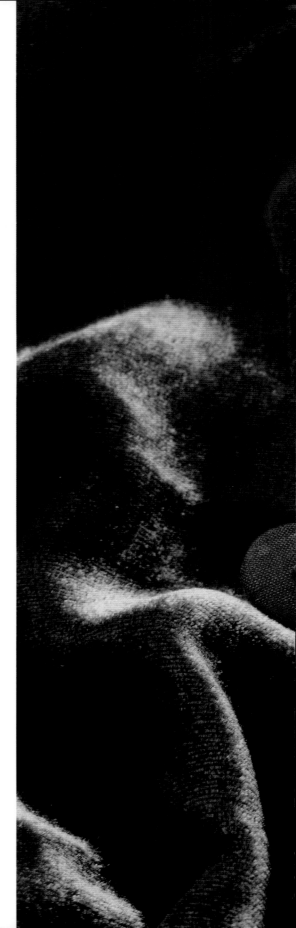

CORD-BEADED BRACELET

CORD BEADING IS VERY POPULAR AMONG THE ZULU PEOPLE OF SOUTH AFRICA, WHO ARE SOME OF THE MOST SKILLED AND PROLIFIC BEAD-WORKERS IN THE WORLD. IT IS A VERY SIMPLE TECHNIQUE, IN WHICH THREADS OF SMALL BEADS ARE WOUND AROUND AND THEN STITCHED ONTO A READY-MADE CORD CORE. THIS BRACELET HAS A BUTTON AND LOOP FASTENING. TO MAKE A BANGLE, BIND THE ENDS OF THE CORD TOGETHER BEFORE BEADING TO MAKE A CONTINUOUS CIRCLE. FOR A NECKLACE OR BELT, SIMPLY EXTEND THE LENGTH OF THE CORD. YOU CAN VARY THE EFFECT BY MIXING BEADS OF DIFFERENT COLORS.

1 Bind both ends of the cord tightly with thread. Paint the cord with fabric paint.

2 Thread the needle and fasten to one end of the cord. Thread on 20 beads, holding thread taut and pushing the beads together. Wind the beads around the cord, make a couple of stitches, then pass the needle back through the last few beads. Repeat along the length of the cord.

3 To finish the ends of the cord, thread on a few beads and make a stitch across the blunt end. Make several more stitches to completely cover the end.

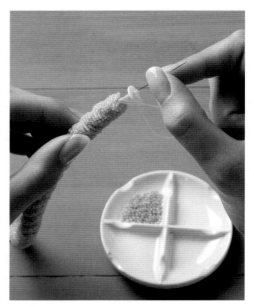

4 Make a beaded loop at one end of the cord (see Basic Techniques). At the other end, thread on three beads, then pass the needle through the button. Thread on two more beads, pass the needle back through the button and make several stitches to finish up.

MATERIALS AND EQUIPMENT YOU WILL NEED

THICK CORD • THREAD • FABRIC PAINT, TO MATCH BEADS • PAINTBRUSH • BEADING NEEDLE • BEADING THREAD • SMALL GLASS BEADS • BUTTON, DIAMETER TO MATCH CORD

SEQUINED CHRISTMAS DECORATIONS

SEQUINS MAKE WONDERFUL CHRISTMAS DECORATIONS, TWINKLING AND SPARKLING AS THEY CATCH THE LIGHT. USE CONCAVE SEQUINS RATHER THAN FLAT ONES, AS THEY WILL GIVE THE FINISHED BAUBLES A SMOOTH SURFACE.

SEQUIN PINS ARE USED TO HOLD THE SEQUINS IN PLACE—BECAUSE THEY ARE SHORTER THAN DRESSMAKER'S PINS, THEY WILL NOT CLOG THE COTTON SPHERE FOUNDATION. THE PINS ALSO GIVE THE BAUBLES A PLEASING WEIGHT.

1 Using a marker, divide the surface of the cotton sphere into quarters, as shown. Mark around the middle of the sphere to divide it into eight sections.

2 Outline the sections with round concave sequins, using different colors. Use sequin pins to attach the sequins and overlap them slightly.

3 Fill in the sections, again overlapping the sequins slightly.

4 Using a beading needle and thread, make several small stitches in the top of the sphere. Thread on 3 inches of small bronze glass beads, then make several more stitches to make a loop for hanging. Thread a metal bead onto a pin and press into the sphere to secure the loop.

5 To make the star bauble, mark several horizontal stripes. Press in a sequin at the top and bottom. Working outward from these points, press in silver pointed sequins to form a star shape.

6 Fill in the rest of sphere with round sequins, as in steps 2 and 3. As an alternative hanging loop, attach a 4-inch piece of ribbon to the top, using a dressmaker's pin and metal bead as in step 4.

MATERIALS AND EQUIPMENT YOU WILL NEED
TWO COMPRESSED COTTON SPHERES, 2½ INCHES IN DIAMETER • MARKER PEN • ¼-INCH DIAMETER ROUND CONCAVE SEQUINS IN A VARIETY OF COLORS, INCLUDING METALLIC • SEQUIN PINS • BEADING NEEDLE • BEADING THREAD • SMALL BRONZE-COLORED GLASS BEADS • FLUTED METAL BEADS • DRESSMAKER'S PINS • SILVER POINTED OVAL SEQUINS • RIBBON

DEVORÉ SCARF

THE LEAF PATTERN ON THIS DEVORÉ VELVET FABRIC IS ECHOED IN APPLIQUÉ AND BEADWORK. SOME LEAF SHAPES ARE CUT OUT OF THE DEVORÉ FABRIC AND FUSED TO THE ORGANZA BACKING; OTHERS ARE STITCHED WITH TINY SEQUINS AND EMBROIDERY THREAD. TO COMPLETE THE EFFECT, BEADED FLOWERS ARE DOTTED AMONG THE LEAVES. THE SCARF IS FINISHED WITH A DRAMATIC SILK BINDING IN A CONTRASTING COLOR.

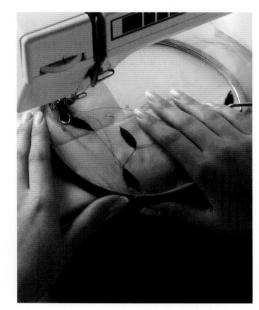

1 Cut an 8 x 8-inch square of devoré velvet. Using a hot iron, fuse the web to the wrong side. Cut out individual leaf shapes from the fabric using embroidery scissors.

2 Peel away the backing paper from the leaf shapes. Scatter them on one end of the organza, right sides up, and fuse in place with a hot iron.

3 Attach a darning foot to the sewing machine and set to darning mode. Place the organza in an embroidery hoop and zigzag-stitch around the edge of each leaf in matching thread.

▶

MATERIALS AND EQUIPMENT YOU WILL NEED

SCISSORS • 11 INCHES OF 52-INCH-WIDE DEVORÉ VELVET, WITH LEAF PATTERN • IRON • FUSIBLE WEB •
EMBROIDERY SCISSORS • 8 INCHES 45-INCH-WIDE ORGANZA • SEWING MACHINE AND DARNING FOOT •
MATCHING THREAD • EMBROIDERY HOOP • FABRIC MARKER • NEEDLE • MATCHING EMBROIDERY THREAD • SMALL SILVER SEQUINS •
SMALL SILVER GLASS BEADS • ¼-INCH BLUE OVAL BEADS • 4 INCHES 45-INCH-WIDE SILK, IN CONTRASTING COLOR

4 Using a fabric marker, draw extra leaves scattered over the scarf.

5 Place the end with the devoré leaves in the embroidery hoop. To fill in the drawn shapes, thread a needle with matching thread and stick it through one end of a leaf. Thread on a sequin, then make a stitch at the side of it. Bring the needle up on the other side, thread on another sequin, then insert the needle in the center of the first sequin. Bring it out on the other side of the second sequin. Overlap the sequins to lie smoothly.

6 Fill in a few of the drawn shapes with small silver beads applied by hand. To make the flowers, stitch a small silver bead in the center of a sequin. Bring the needle out on one side of the sequin, then thread on a silver bead, a blue bead and another silver bead. Insert the needle in the fabric and bring out on the other side of the sequin. Stitch five more petals around the sequin.

7 Cut a piece of devoré fabric 11 x 45 inches. With the wrong sides together, machine-stitch to the organza on all four sides. Cut strips of contrasting silk fabric 1¼ inches wide, stitch together and press to make a continuous binding. With the right sides together, stitch all around the scarf. Fold the binding over the edge of the scarf, tuck under the raw edges and slip-stitch.

Above: Devoré velvet never dates and has a subtle elegance that is very flattering.

WOVEN BRACELET

INSPIRED BY THE DESIGNS OF THE ART DECO MOVEMENT, THE DESIGNER HAS CHOSEN PEARLIZED ICE-CREAM COLORS IN A GEOMETRIC PATTERN. THE PIECE IS WORKED IN SMALL GLASS BEADS ON A BEAD LOOM. AS WHEN WEAVING FABRICS, THE WARP THREADS (VERTICAL THREADS) ARE STRETCHED TAUT, WHILE THE WEFT THREADS (HORIZONTAL THREADS) PASS BACKWARD AND FORWARD UNDER AND OVER THE WARP. LONG, NARROW BRAIDS CAN BE PRODUCED WITH THESE LOOMS.

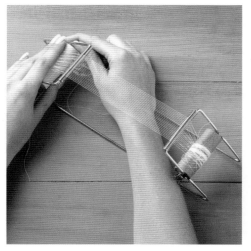

1 Measure the diameter of your wrist to determine the length of your bracelet, and add an extra 18 inches. Cut 21 warp threads to the total length. Lay out the threads and knot together at each end. Divide evenly into two strands. Slip one knot over the roller rivets. Wind on a little thread by turning the roller, then spread the threads out and arrange them in the spring next to each other.

2 Slip the knot at the other end of the warp over the rivets in the other roller and wind on. Wind the rollers on to adjust the tension—the warp threads should be taut.

3 Thread a beading needle with a long thread and draw the thread through beeswax. Tie the other end of the thread to the far-left warp thread 1 inch from the rollers. ▶

MATERIALS AND EQUIPMENT YOU WILL NEED

BEAD LOOM • BEADING THREAD • SCISSORS • BEADING NEEDLE • BEESWAX • SMALL LIGHT GREEN, PINK, GRAY AND PURPLE GLASS BEADS •
ADHESIVE TAPE • WOOL LINING FABRIC • SEWING NEEDLE • THREAD • THREE BUTTONS WITH SHANKS

4 Following the pattern in the template section at the back of the book, thread on 20 beads. Push them up as far as they will go, fitting them in place between the warp threads. With the forefinger push the beads through the spaces, passing the needle back through the beads in the opposite direction above the warp thread. Pull the thread tight. Thread on 20 more beads and continue along the warp in the same way.

5 To finish, pass the needle back through several rows of beads, tie a knot and trim the thread.

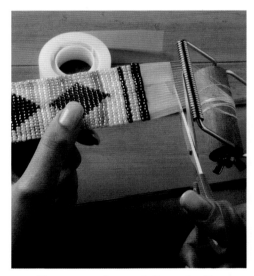

6 To remove the work from the loom, cut two pieces of tape and stick in place over the warp threads at either end of the work. Cut the threads.

7 Cut a piece of wool lining fabric to the same size as the finished work. Tuck the free warp edges under and assemble the work and the lining with the wrong sides together. Work a slip stitch all around the finished piece.

8 On one end of the bracelet, stitch three buttons at equal distances, and on the other end make three beaded loops large enough to fit over the buttons.

WALLET

THE BIRD MOTIF ON THIS ATTRACTIVE WALLET IS MADE FROM BLUE SILK EMBELLISHED WITH SATIN AND RUNNING STITCH. INTERESTING FRAGMENTS OF DRIFTWOOD PROVIDE SOME TEXTURAL CONTRAST AND WORK EXTREMELY WELL WITH THE OVERALL THEME. GOLD CORD, METALLIC EMBROIDERY THREADS AND A SELECTION OF BEADS HELP TO CREATE AN OBJET D'ART THAT, WHEN FINISHED, WILL LOOK AS VALUABLE AS ITS CONTENTS.

1 Draw the bird design and make a cardboard template. For the top side, cut a piece of silk 18 x 6 inches. Fold the fabric in thirds lengthwise and draw around the template. Cut pieces of driftwood and arrange them across the bird shape. Using matching thread, couch the wood in place.

2 Cut a length of gold cord and wind back and forth across the shape, couching it in place with red embroidery thread. Stitch small red beads and other beads to the design. Work a satin stitch for the beak and a running stitch around the shape.

3 For the underside, cut an 18 x 6-inch piece of silk. To stiffen the wallet, cut an 18 x 6-inch piece of heavyweight

interfacing. Cut two pieces of fusible web to the same size. Fuse in place on either side of the interfacing with a hot iron. Remove the paper back. Fold the piece into thirds lengthwise. Fuse underside piece in place.

4 Turn the work over and fuse the topside piece, carefully ironing around the embroidered and beaded area. For the pocket, cut two pieces each of silk and fusible web and one of interfacing, 6 x 6 inches, and bond together as before. Place the pocket at one end of the wallet on the underside and pin. Work a decorative zigzag stitch all around the edge.

MATERIALS AND EQUIPMENT YOU WILL NEED

PENCIL • CARDBOARD • SCISSORS • TAPE MEASURE • BLUE DUPION SILK, APPROXIMATELY 20 INCH X 20 INCHES • FABRIC MARKER • SMALL PIECES OF DRIFTWOOD • CRAFT KNIFE • NEEDLE • THICK COTTON THREAD • GOLD CORD • EMBROIDERY NEEDLE • RED, PURPLE AND SILVER METALLIC EMBROIDERY THREAD • SMALL RED GLASS BEADS • RED BEAD • SILVER BEAD • LARGE GOLD BEADS • HEART BEAD • BRASS BEAD • HEAVYWEIGHT INTERFACING • FUSIBLE WEB • IRON • PINS • SEWING MACHINE AND MATCHING THREADS

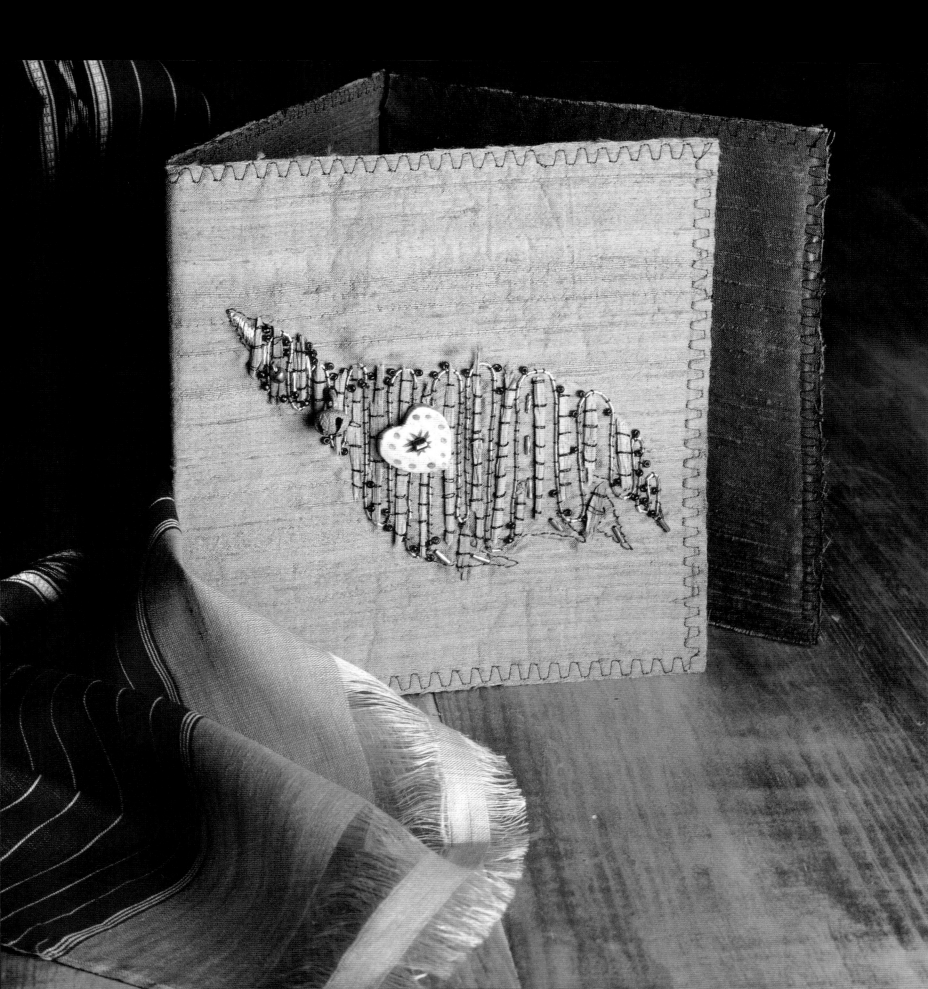

DRAMATIC PAINTED GLOVES

THESE GLOVES ARE PAINTED WITH VIBRANT RED SHOE DYE, AND THEN A FREE-HAND DESIGN IS PICKED OUT WITH TINY BEADS. THE BEADS ARE SEWN ON INDIVIDUALLY, SO THIS IS A VERY EASY FIRST PROJECT FOR A BEGINNER. YOU NEED A STRONG, SHARP NEEDLE TO STITCH THROUGH THE LEATHER; ALTERNATIVELY, YOU CAN USE FABRIC GLOVES. DO NOT EXTEND THE DESIGN TOO FAR DOWN THE GLOVE, AS IT WILL BE DIFFICULT TO SEW.

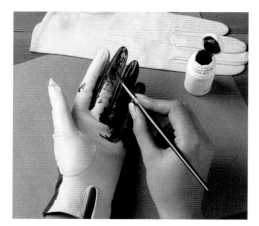

1 Put each glove on to prevent it from shrinking. Paint on the red dye and let dry.

3 Thread the needle with nylon filament. Stitch green beads individually in a row along the cuff edge of each glove.

5 Stitch individual red glass beads at random intervals over the back of the gloves as shown.

2 Draw an abstract design freehand on the back of each glove, using a fabric marker. Start from the cuff end.

4 Stitch more green beads along the lines of the design.

6 Outline the remainder of the design with gold beads. Fill in the shapes with pink beads.

MATERIALS AND EQUIPMENT YOU WILL NEED

LIGHTWEIGHT LEATHER GLOVES • RED LEATHER SHOE DYE • PAINTBRUSH • FABRIC MARKER • FINE LEATHER NEEDLE • NYLON FILAMENT •
SMALL GREEN, RED, GOLD AND PINK GLASS BEADS

PEARL TIARA

THIS PRETTY TIARA IS HEAVILY ENCRUSTED WITH SPIRALS OF ARTIFICIAL PEARLS TO MAKE A SCALLOPED EDGE. THE DESIGNER HAS ATTACHED DIFFERENT-SIZE BEADS ONTO A BACKING STIFFENED WITH WIRE. THE TIARA MAY BE STITCHED TO A USEFUL COMB OR HAIR CLIP. IT WOULD BE AN IDEAL HAIR ADORNMENT FOR A BRIDE TO HOLD A VEIL IN PLACE. FOR BRIDESMAIDS, CHOOSE FROM A WIDE RANGE OF PEARLIZED COLORS INSTEAD OF IVORY.

1 Trace the template from the back of the book onto cardboard and cut out. Mark around the template twice on the heavyweight interfacing and cut out.

2 Bend a loop at each end of the millinery wire. Stitch the wire to one piece of the interfacing ¼ inch from the straight edge.

3 Following the template guide, mark the center of each scallop on the right side of the wire-stiffened interfacing. Stitch the largest bead of ½ inch to the center of the middle scallop. Bring the needle through to the right side next to the last bead and thread on approximately eight ¼-inch beads and enough ⅓-inch beads to spiral outward to fill the scallop shape, then make a fastening stitch to secure.

4 Thread a sewing needle with matching thread and make tiny stitches over the beading thread in between the pearl beads. Repeat for the other scallops using ⅖-inch beads in the center of each. Couch down the small beads to fill in the remaining interfacing.

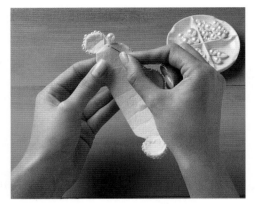

5 Stitch the back piece of the tiara to the front with a slip stitch. Stitch the drop beads between the scallops.

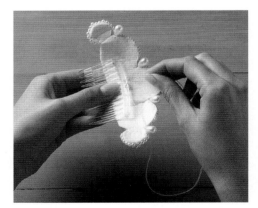

6 Stitch the comb on the wrong side to the bottom edge of the beaded piece.

MATERIALS AND EQUIPMENT YOU WILL NEED

CARDBOARD • PENCIL • CRAFT KNIFE • HEAVYWEIGHT INTERFACING • FABRIC MARKER • EMBROIDERY SCISSORS • 7 INCHES MILLINERY WIRE • JEWELRY PLIERS • SEWING NEEDLE • MATCHING THREAD • BEADING NEEDLE • MATCHING BEADING THREAD • ONE LARGE PEARL BEAD, ½ INCH • MEDIUM-SIZED PEARLS, ¼ INCH • SMALL PEARLS, ⅓ INCH • FOUR LARGE PEARL BEADS, ⅖ INCH • DROP BEADS • PLASTIC HAIR COMB

BEAD-TRIMMED CUSHIONS

THE SIMPLEST CUSHION CAN BE DRAMATICALLY TRANSFORMED WITH A BEAD-WORK EDGING. THESE THREE DESIGNS SHOW HOW BEADS OF DIFFERENT WEIGHTS AND SIZES GIVE DIFFERENT EFFECTS. SMALL BEADS MAKE A BEAUTIFULLY DELICATE FRINGE, WHILE LARGE GLASS BEADS GIVE A MUCH FIRMER, BOLD EDGE. CHOOSE BEADS TO CONTRAST OR TO BLEND SUBTLY WITH THE FABRIC. MEASURE THE SIZE OF CUSHION PAD REQUIRED AND ALLOW EXTRA FABRIC FOR THE COVER.

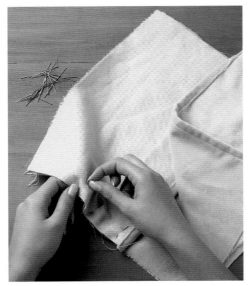

1 For the yellow cushion with bead border: To make the the front cover, cut one piece of velvet the size of the cushion pad plus a ¾-inch seam allowance all around. For the back cover, cut two pieces of velvet the same width and two-thirds the length. Press under a double hem on both short sides of the back cover and machine-stitch. With right sides facing and the stitched edges overlapping, pin the front and back covers together. Machine-stitch all around. Turn right side out.

2 Thread beading needle with doubled sewing thread. Make several fastening-on stitches in the seam at one corner. Working from left to right, thread on two white glass beads, one yellow bead and one copper bead. Pass the needle back through the yellow bead and thread on two white glass beads. Insert the needle into the seam ¾ inch to the right.

3 Make a tiny stitch, then thread on a blue or white opaque bead and a copper bead. Pass the needle back through the blue or white bead, then insert the needle ¾ inch further on. Repeat the sequence all around the cover.

MATERIALS AND EQUIPMENT YOU WILL NEED

TAPE MEASURE • SQUARE CUSHION PAD • SCISSORS • YELLOW VELVET • IRON • SEWING MACHINE AND MATCHING THREAD • DRESSMAKER'S PINS • BEADING NEEDLE • MATCHING THREAD • ¼-INCH WHITE GLASS BEADS • ½-INCH OPAQUE YELLOW BEADS • SMALL COPPER-COLORED GLASS BEADS • ½-INCH OPAQUE WHITE BEADS • ½-INCH OPAQUE BLUE BEADS • RECTANGULAR CUSHION PAD • STRIPED FABRIC • FABRIC MARKER • GRAPH PAPER • PENCIL • SMALL PINK AND YELLOW GLASS BEADS • ½-INCH YELLOW DISK-SHAPED BEADS • RECTANGULAR CUSHION PAD • PINK VELVET • SMALL YELLOW AND PINK GLASS BEADS • ¼-INCH WHITE GLASS BEADS • ¼-INCH TURQUOISE GLASS BEADS • SMALL COPPER-COLORED GLASS BEADS

4 For the striped cushion with fringe: To make the front cover, cut a piece of fabric the size of the cushion pad plus ¾ inch on the width and 8 inches on the length. For the back, cut two pieces the same width as the front and two-thirds the length. Press under a double hem on the short back opening edges and machine-stitch. With right sides facing and stitched edges overlapping, pin and stitch length-wise seam. Turn right side out and press. Mark a line 4 inches from raw edges on both sides and topstitch. Carefully pull away the fabric close to the stitching. Starting from the outer edges, separate and remove threads up to the line.

5 Mark the desired length of fringe, 4 inches, on graph paper. Cut thread four times this measurement and double through the needle. Insert the needle at the inner edge of the first stripe of the fabric and secure with a knot, pass the needle through the loop and pull taut.

7 For the pink lattice-trimmed cushion: Make up the velvet cover as in step 1. Mark points ½ inch apart along two opposite sides.

6 Mix a few pink with the yellow beads. Thread on 3¾ inches of beads, using graph paper as a guide. Thread on a disk and a small yellow bead. Pass the needle back through the disk, make a finishing stitch, pass the needle up the strand and make another finishing stitch. Pull gently on the strand to iron out kinks. Trim thread. Repeat with the other stripes.

8 Repeat this sequence along the length of the cushion. Sew several tiny stitches into the seam at one corner. Mix a few yellow with the pink beads, thread on ¾ inch. Add one white bead, and ¾ inch of pink or yellow and one turquoise and one copper bead. Using the copper bead as an anchor, pass needle back through turquoise bead, thread on ¾ inch pink or yellow, a large white, then more pink or yellow. Insert needle into velvet at the third marked point. ▶

9 Make a backstitch to bring the needle out at the second marked point. Thread on ¾ inch of pink or yellow beads, then pass the needle through the white bead already in place.

10 Thread on another ¾ inch of pink or yellow beads, one turquoise and one copper bead. Repeat the lattice sequence along each side of the cushion.

VELVET BOLSTER CUSHION

WIRE ADDS BODY TO EVEN THE FINEST BEADWORK AND IS THEREFORE IDEAL FOR FURNISHING PROJECTS THAT REQUIRE NEAT EDGES AND FRINGES. IN THIS DRAMATIC BOLSTER, SMALL GLASS BEADS IN A STRONGLY CONTRASTING COLOR ARE THREADED ONTO WIRE AND THEN INTO THE VELVET FABRIC TO CREATE THREE-DIMENSIONAL CURLING TENDRILS. THE FINE BEADING WIRE ACTS IN THE SAME WAY AS A NEEDLE AND THREAD TO "STITCH" THROUGH THE FABRIC.

1 Measure the diameter of the end of the bolster cushion and divide in half to find the radius. Draw a circle to this size on paper, using a compass, then redraw, adding a ½-inch seam allowance. Cut two circles in velvet.

2 Measure the length and circumference of the bolster. Cut a piece of embossed velvet to this size plus a 1¼-inch seam allowance all around.

3 Tie one end of a piece of beading wire in a knot and pass through the center of a velvet circle to the right side. Thread on red beads for 4 inches. Insert the end of the wire back into the velvet 1¼ inches from the knot to make a loop. ▶

MATERIALS AND EQUIPMENT YOU WILL NEED

BOLSTER CUSHION PAD • TAPE MEASURE • COMPASS • PENCIL AND PAPER • SCISSORS • 20 INCHES OF 39-INCH-WIDE BLUE-BLACK EMBOSSED VELVET • 0.2 MM BEADING WIRE • SMALL RED GLASS BEADS • SEWING NEEDLE • MATCHING THREAD • SEWING MACHINE AND MATCHING THREADS • DRESSMAKER'S PINS

4 Thread the wire through the fabric again 2 inches from the first loop. Make a second loop as before. Repeat until there are about 20 loops, using extra wire as needed. Fasten the wire securely. Repeat for the second circle.

5 Run a gathering stitch around each circle, using matching sewing thread.

6 With right sides together, fold the large piece of embossed velvet in half lengthwise. Machine-stitch the long edge, leaving a ½-inch seam. Leave a gap large enough to insert the cushion pad.

7 Insert the cushion pad and pin and slip stitch the gap.

Above: The finished bolster cushion feels as luxurious as it looks.

DRAWSTRING BAG

Inspired by ethnic beadwork, this attractive little bag is made of traditional ikat fabric from Indonesia, lined with a contrasting plain fabric. The lining also acts as a binding and casing for the shoelace drawstring ties. The bag is quilted with a running stitch, then decorated with a pointed beadwork fringe that echoes the diagonal pattern of the stitching. This is an ideal project for a newcomer to beadwork.

1 Cut the ikat fabric into two 6-inch-square pieces. On the right side of each piece, mark a line diagonally from corner to corner in both directions, then mark parallel lines ¾ inch apart.

2 Trace a bag shape similar to the bag in the finished picture and transfer to cardboard. Lay the cardboard template on both pieces of ikat fabric and cut out. Cut two pieces of plain fabric 6¼ x 8 inches for the lining. With the marked lines right side up, baste one bag piece to each lining piece. Using a running stitch, stitch along the lines. Trim the excess lining fabric.

3 To make the casing, cut two pieces of lining fabric 2¾ x 4¾ inches. Press in half lengthwise, then press in a ½-inch turning all around. Pin one long edge to the top of the bag as shown and machine-stitch. Repeat with the second casing.

▶

MATERIALS AND EQUIPMENT YOU WILL NEED
SCISSORS • 12 x 6 INCHES IKAT FABRIC • TRIANGLE OR RULER • FABRIC MARKER • PENCIL AND PAPER •
THIN CARDBOARD • 14 x 14 INCHES PLAIN-COLORED FABRIC, IN CONTRASTING COLOR • IRON • DRESSMAKER'S PINS •
SEWING MACHINE AND MATCHING THREAD • NEEDLE AND THREAD TO MATCH LINING • BEADING NEEDLE • BLACK STRANDED EMBROIDERY FLOSS •
SMALL BLACK GLASS BEADS • SMALL MULTICOLORED GLASS BEADS • TWO 20-INCH BLACK SHOELACES • 12 LARGE BEADS WITH LARGE HOLES

4 Place the two bag pieces right sides together. Pin, then machine-stitch ½ inch from the raw edges. Leave the top open.

5 Turn the bag right side out. Fold the casings over the raw edges and slip-stitch in place.

6 Thread a beading needle with stranded embroidery floss and stick it through one end of the machine-stitched seam line. Thread on seven black beads and one colored bead, then pass the needle back through the last black bead. Thread on six more black beads and make a small stitch along the seam line ½ inch to the side. Repeat all around the seam line.

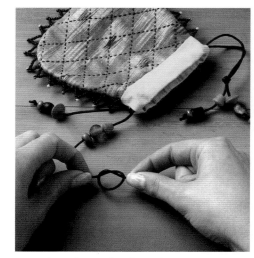

7 Thread one shoelace through each casing for the drawstring. Thread three large beads onto the end of each shoelace and knot. Tie the two shoelaces together at either end.

CHILD'S SLIPPERS

A TINY PAIR OF CHILD'S SLIPPERS ARE EMBROIDERED WITH A GOLDEN STREAM OF BUGLE BEADS. INSTEAD OF STITCHING THE BEADS INDIVIDUALLY, A STRING OF BUGLE BEADS IS LAID ACROSS EACH SLIPPER AND A SECOND THREAD IS STITCHED OVER IT TO COUCH DOWN THE BEADS. THE TEMPLATES AT THE BACK OF THE BOOK ARE FOR THE LEFT SLIPPER; REVERSE THEM FOR THE RIGHT SLIPPER. FOR LARGER SIZES, YOU CAN SCALE UP THE TEMPLATES ON A PHOTOCOPIER.

1 For each slipper, cut four pieces of blue wool to the size of the back template, then stitch the back seam together. Assemble each pair with the right sides together and stitch the back seam. Work a zigzag stitch along the top and bottom edges. Set the sewing machine to darning mode and attach darning foot. Stitch wavy lines over the piece to quilt it.

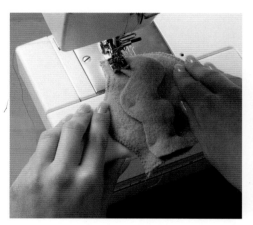

2 To make the bias binding, fold a velvet square in half diagonally, unfold and mark the fold line. Mark parallel lines across the cloth 1¼ inches apart. Cut along the lines. Match the raw edges of bias binding to the top edge of the back piece. Stitch the binding ¼ inch from edge, fold bias binding over and tuck under raw edges. Slip-stitch in place.

3 Cut one piece of fabric to the size of the template for the toe piece. Stitch the dart. Cut out the template for the beaded appliqué piece, and pin it to the toe as shown. Work a zigzag stitch around the appliqué.

4 Stitch 12 inches of bias binding to the top edge of the toe piece, and fold in half. Pin the fold to the center front edge of the toe piece. Pin all around the front and stitch ¼ inch from the raw edges. ▶

MATERIALS AND EQUIPMENT YOU WILL NEED

PAPER AND PENCIL • SCISSORS • 20 X 20 INCHES PALE BLUE WOOL FABRIC • SEWING MACHINE AND DARNING FOOT •
MATCHING SEWING THREADS • 12 X 12 INCHES DARK GRAY VELVET • FABRIC MARKER • SEWING NEEDLE AND MATCHING THREAD • DRESSMAKER'S
PINS • BEADING NEEDLE • BEADING THREAD • GOLD BUGLE BEADS • 8 X 8 INCHES GRAY WOOL FABRIC •
8 X 8 INCHES BATTING

5 At the top edge of the appliquéd piece, make a few stitches, then thread on enough bugle beads to follow the line of the piece and insert the beading needle at the other side.

7 Completely cover the appliquéd piece with rows of couching that follow the contours of the first row of beads.

9 Match the center back to the center heel of the sole, and pin the back piece around the sole. Pin and machine-stitch ¼ inch from the edge. Pin the toe piece in place over the front, and machine-stitch. Stitch the sides of the toe piece to the back where they meet. Pin the bias binding around the base of the back of the slipper, turn both ends under at the center back, and slip-stitch the seam. Fold the bias binding over the edge of the sole, and slip-stitch in place on the underside.

6 Thread a second needle, make tiny stitches over the laid thread between the first and second bead, push the third bead up close and make another couching stitch between that and the fourth bead.

8 For each slipper, cut two pieces of gray wool fabric and one of batting to the size of the template. Assemble the batting between the wool pieces. Set the sewing machine to darning mode and attach a darning foot, then stitch a wavy line to quilt the layers. Work a wide zigzag stitch around the edge.

BOTTLE COLLAR

THIS EXQUISITE DECORATION IS MADE BY NEEDLE-WOVEN BEADING (SEE BASIC TECHNIQUES). IT CREATES AN OPENWORK STRUCTURE SIMILAR TO LACE BUT, ALTHOUGH THE RESULT LOOKS INTRICATE, THE TECHNIQUE IS VERY SIMPLE. USING A NEEDLE AND THREAD, EACH ROUND OF BEADS IS WOVEN INTO THE PREVIOUS ROUND, WITH THE SECOND ROUND FITTING BETWEEN PAIRS OF THE FIRST. THE NUMBER OF BEADS IN EACH ROUND INCREASES SO THAT THE COLLAR EXPANDS TO COVER THE TOP OF THE BOTTLE WITH A HONEYCOMB NET OF BEADS. THE COMBINATION OF RED, GREEN, PURPLE AND SILVER WOULD LOOK GREAT AT CHRISTMAS.

1 Begin by threading an even number of light green beads onto a long length of thread. This gives you round 1 of the collar. Tie around the neck of the bottle and tie knots at the ends.

2 For round 2, pass the needle through the first bead of round 1, add a red bead, then pass it through alternate light green beads. Continue to thread a red bead between each pair of green beads. Pass the needle through the first red bead of this round to begin round 3.

3 For round 3, thread a light green bead between each pair of red beads. Pass the needle through the first light green bead of this round to begin round 4.

4 For round 4, thread an oval bead, a light green bead and another oval bead, then pass the needle through the second light green bead of round 3 to create loops. ▶

MATERIALS AND EQUIPMENT YOU WILL NEED

BEADING NEEDLE • BEADING THREAD • ¼-INCH LIGHT GREEN ROUND GLASS BEADS • GLASS BOTTLE, WITH CORK STOPPER • ¼-INCH RED DIAMOND GLASS BEADS • ¼-INCH BRIGHT GREEN OVAL GLASS BEADS • SMALL PURPLE GLASS BEADS • SMALL SILVER BEADS • EIGHT LARGE DROP BEADS WITH SILVER FOIL INSERTS • SCISSORS • SEQUIN PINS

5 For round 5, thread the following beads: three purple, one light green, one red, one light green, six purple, one light green, one red, one silver. Pass the needle back through the red and light green beads, then thread on seven purple, one light green, one red, one light green and three purple beads.

6 Pass the needle through the third light green bead of round 4. Repeat in sequence all around the collar. Pass the needle through the first light green bead of the round, then through an oval bead, a light green bead and another oval bead. Pass the needle through the second light green bead to begin the sequence again.

7 For round 6, thread on three purple beads and one light green bead through red beads of round 5. Add one light green, nine purple, one light green, one large drop, one red and one silver bead. Pass needle back through preceding three beads: red, drop and light green. Thread on nine purple beads and one light green, then pass needle through the red bead of round 5. Thread on one light green and three purple beads, then pass needle through fourth light green bead of round 4. Repeat the sequence. Pull up thread tightly and tie a knot. Pass needle through several beads and snip the thread.

8 Thread a silver bead and a red bead on each sequin pin, then press them into the cork at an angle so that they fan out at the edge. Pin a silver bead and a large drop into the center of the cork stopper.

BEAD CANDLEHOLDER

To make a three-dimensional object, beads are threaded onto wire and wound around a frame that is constructed over a solid form and removed at the end. Bowls can also be made in the same way.

Inexpensive glass beads look very effective in this stylish modern design. The restrained shades of gray, white and gold come to life in the glow of candlelight. A large night-light will fit comfortably inside the frame.

1 Cut two pieces of 0.6 mm wire twice the height and diameter of the glass plus 4 inches. Twist the wires together at their halfway points, then tape the knot to the center of the glass base. Slip a rubber band over the glass to hold the wire in place. Fold ends over lip of the glass.

2 Cut two pieces of 0.2 mm wire approximately 39 inches long. Find their halfway points, then twist both pieces around the knot on the base of the glass. Wrap each wire around your hand to prevent it from becoming entangled.

3 Thread the gray glass beads onto the 0.6 mm gold wire.

4 To begin the winding wire, use the pliers to wind one end of the remainder of the thicker wire into a flat spiral ¾ inch across. Secure at the center of the base by weaving the thinner wire over and under the frame and the spiraled wire.

5 Thread more gray beads onto winding wire and continue to wind it into a spiral, weaving the thinner wire under and over frame. Continue up the sides of the glass to within ½ inch of the top.

6 Remove rubber band. To make a lip, ease the top of the frame outward and thread on white beads. Continue to weave the thinner wire under and over the winding wire and the frame. Thread on small gold beads. Open out ends of frame, remove glass, trim ends and fold back over. Using thinner wire, secure the ends to frame.

MATERIALS AND EQUIPMENT YOU WILL NEED

WIRE CUTTERS • 0.6 MM GOLD WIRE • GLASS TUMBLER • ADHESIVE TAPE • LARGE RUBBER BAND • 0.2 MM GOLD WIRE • ROUND-NOSED
JEWELRY PLIERS • ¼-INCH GRAY GLASS BEADS • ¼-INCH WHITE GLASS BEADS • ¼-INCH GOLD-COLORED GLASS BEADS

CREAMER COVER

BRODERIE ANGLAISE AND BEADS ARE A TRADITIONAL COMBINATION, THE BEADS ENHANCING THE DELICATE PATTERN OF THE TRIM. HEAVY GLASS BEADS ALSO PROVIDE THE WEIGHT THE MUSLIN COVER NEEDS TO HANG NICELY. YOU CAN MAKE A LARGER COVER FOR SUMMER ENTERTAINING WITH PITCHERS OF HOMEMADE LEMONADE OR CIDER. THE SAME IDEA WOULD ALSO LOOK VERY PRETTY USED TO WEIGHT MUSLIN CURTAINS OR AS A SHELF EDGING.

1 Draw around the saucer on the muslin. Cut out, leaving an extra ½-inch hem allowance all around. Turn under a single hem and baste.

2 Run a gathering stitch along the top edge of the broderie anglaise and draw up to fit the muslin. Slip-stitch the broderie anglaise onto the muslin hem, turning under the raw edges and stitching them together. Trim excess muslin hem.

3 Thread the needle with beading thread. Stitch a row of alternate pale and dark green beads around the edge of the muslin.

4 Fasten the thread on at the point of a scallop in the broderie anglaise. Thread two pink beads, one green heart, one pink, two dark green, three pale green, five white, one Venetian, five white, two pale green, two dark green, one pink, one green heart and two pink.

5 Insert the needle at another scallop point, then pass the needle back through the last two pink beads and green heart to make a loop. Continue this sequence all around the edge. Picking out the delicate patterns in the broderie anglaise, stitch tiny flowers. Stitch two rows of four pink beads next to each other with a dark green bead in the center.

MATERIALS AND EQUIPMENT YOU WILL NEED
FABRIC MARKER • SMALL SAUCER • APPROXIMATELY 8 x 8 INCHES MUSLIN, TO FIT SAUCER • SCISSORS • FINE NEEDLE •
MATCHING THREADS • 20 INCHES NARROW BRODERIE ANGLAISE • BEADING THREAD • SMALL ¼-INCH GLASS BEADS: PALE GREEN,
DARK GREEN, WHITE AND PINK • GREEN HEART-SHAPED BEADS • ¼-INCH WHITE VENETIAN BEADS

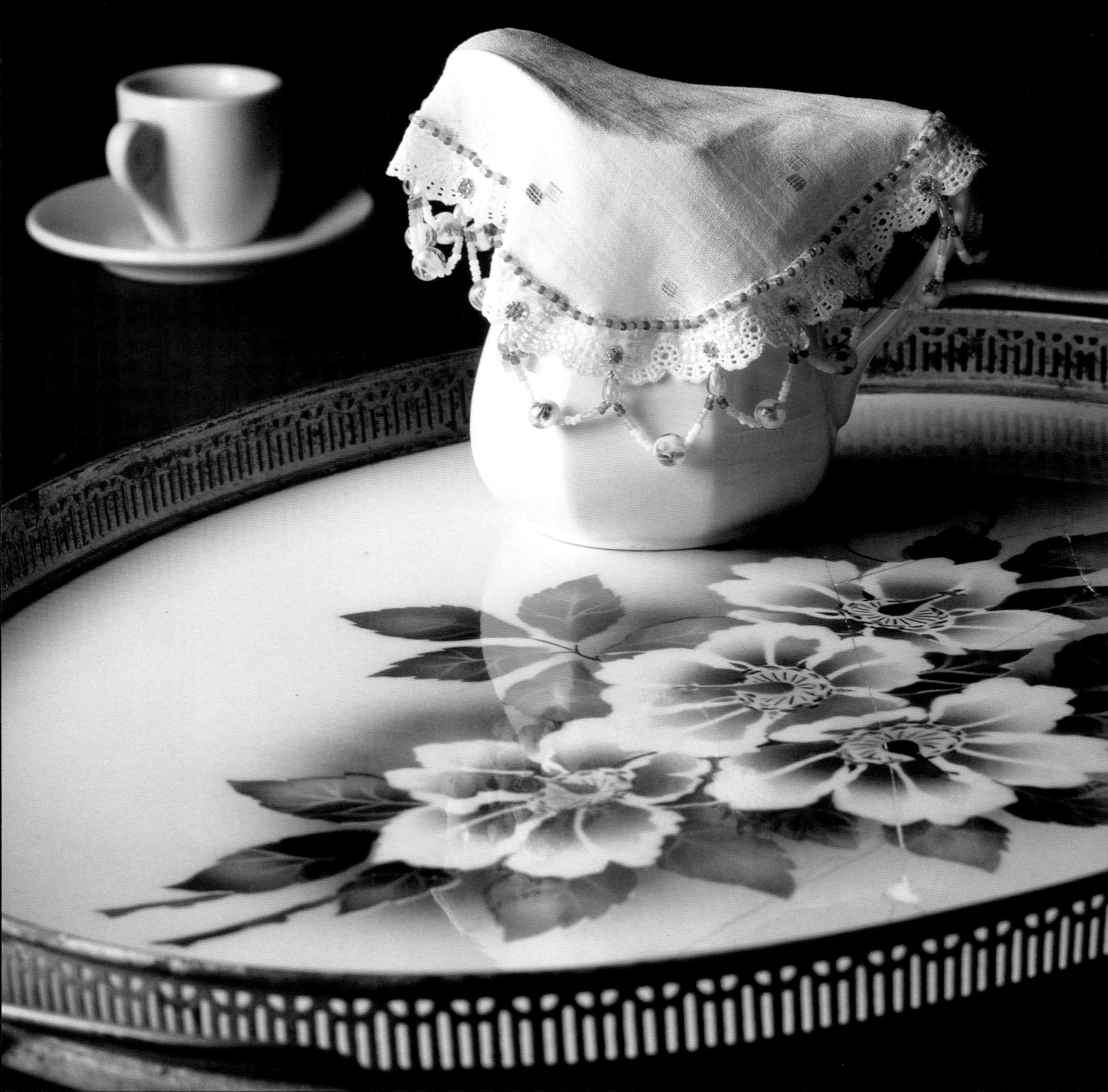

NEEDLEPOINT PHOTOGRAPH ALBUM

HERE A TRADITIONAL VICTORIAN CRAFT HAS BEEN BROUGHT UP TO DATE WITH A STRIKING MODERN DESIGN. THE GLOSSY BEADWORK CONTRASTS BEAUTIFULLY WITH THE MATTE WOOL YARNS USED TO COVER THE BACKGROUND. THIS TECHNIQUE WAS VERY POPULAR IN THE NINETEENTH CENTURY FOR TEA COSIES, CUSHIONS AND CHAIR COVERS. USE THICK BLACK PAPER FOR A PHOTOGRAPH ALBUM, OR LIGHTER-WEIGHT CREAM OR WHITE PAPER FOR A SPECIAL DIARY OR DAYBOOK.

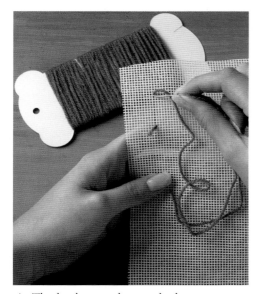

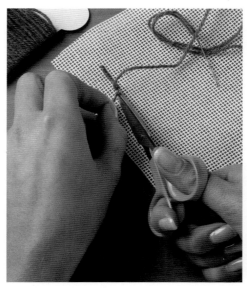

1 The background is worked in a tent stitch. Double a length of tapestry yarn through the needle and knot the ends together. Insert the needle from the right side into the canvas and bring it out ¾ inch to the left. To make a stitch, insert the needle into the hole diagonally below and to the right, then bring it out of the hole immediately above.

2 Work a few stitches until the end of the yarn is covered, then snip off the knot.

3 Continue stitching in rows, following the chart at the back of the book. Leave a wide border all around and gaps for the beadwork motifs. Merge the shades of green as shown. ▶

MATERIALS AND EQUIPMENT YOU WILL NEED

TAPESTRY YARN IN SHADES OF GREEN • TAPESTRY NEEDLE • 19 x 13½ INCHES TAPESTRY CANVAS, 10 HOLES TO 1 INCH • EMBROIDERY SCISSORS • BEADING NEEDLE • MATCHING BEADING THREAD • 1/16-INCH GLASS BEADS: COPPER, LIGHT BLUE, GOLD, SILVER AND BLACK • CRAFT KNIFE AND RULER • CARDBOARD • BOOKBINDING FABRIC • PAPER GLUE • ADHESIVE TAPE • BLACK OR WHITE PAPER • HOLE PUNCH • PAIR OF BRASS SCREW BINDERS

4 Thread the beading needle with beading thread. Stitch on the beads one by one, making a tent stitch in the opposite direction to the wool stitches—the beads will then lie in the same direction as the wool stitches.

6 Complete the beadwork, following the chart at the back of the book and using different colors of beads.

8 For the front cover, lay the embroidery on the second piece of cardboard, lining up the right-hand sides. Stretch canvas over cardboard and tape edges to the wrong side. Tape the left-hand side of the embroidery to the front of the cardboard. Cut a piece of fabric 4¾ inches x the width of the cardboard plus 1½ inch. Match to the edge of the embroidery and glue in place. Fold the fabric edges over the cardboard and glue down. Line the front cover just like the back.

5 Every four or five stitches, make two securing stitches to prevent the beads from unraveling.

7 Cut two pieces of cardboard the same size as the finished embroidery plus 4 inches on the length. Score a line 4 inches from the left-hand short edge on both pieces. To make the back cover, cut a piece of bookbinding fabric the same size as the cardboard plus ¾ inch all around and clip the corners. Glue the paper backing and press onto the cardboard. Fold over the edges and glue down. To make a lining, cut a second piece of bookbinding fabric the size of the cardboard and glue inside the back cover.

9 Cut 40 pieces of paper ½ inch less all around than the cardboard. Mark position of the holes on the back and front covers and the paper, then punch holes. Place paper between the two covers, thread screws through layers and secure.

SPIRALED "CHANDELIER"

IN THIS DELICATE MODERN VERSION OF A TRADITIONAL GLASS CHANDELIER, DROPLETS OF COLORED GLASS HANG AND QUIVER FROM A SIMPLE STRUCTURE OF SPIRALED WIRE. SUSPEND THE CHANDELIER FROM THE CEILING WITH A LENGTH OF STRONG FISHING TWINE. TO SHOW IT TO BEST ADVANTAGE, PLACE IT IN FRONT OF A WINDOW OR CAREFULLY OVER A HANGING LIGHT SO THAT THE LIGHT SHINES THROUGH THE BEADS.

1 Using wire cutters, cut two lengths of the thick wire 47 inches long. Bend each piece into a spiral.

2 Using the pliers, bend a small loop at each end of both pieces of wire.

3 Assemble the two spirals of wire together, as shown. ▶

MATERIALS AND EQUIPMENT YOU WILL NEED
WIRE CUTTERS • 100 INCHES OF 2 MM WIRE • ROUND-NOSED JEWELRY PLIERS • 0.2 MM WIRE •
SELECTION OF SPHERICAL AND FACETED GLASS AND PLASTIC BEADS • SMALL GLASS BEADS • ¼-INCH BUGLE BEADS

4 To make the droplets, thread a piece of thin wire through a large glass spherical bead and a small bead—the small bead will act as an anchor. Pass the wire back through the beads and twist the ends together.

5 Thread on some bugle beads, then twist the wires to make a stem. Make about 30 droplets, using different beads in different arrangements.

6 Wind a short piece of wire onto each stem. Bend the ends into hooks, using the pliers.

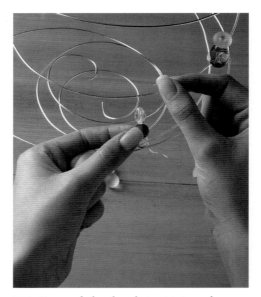

7 Suspend the droplets at intervals on the spiral frame.

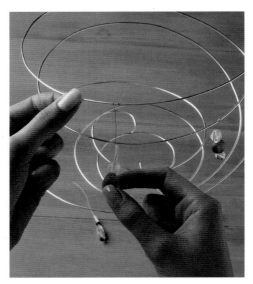

8 To hold the spiral shape, some of the droplets should be twisted over two rounds of the spiral.

9 Finish by adding glass beads to the ends of the spiral frame.

FLOWERED FRAME

DECEPTIVELY FRAGILE THREE-DIMENSIONAL STRUCTURES CAN BE MADE BY SIMPLY THREADING BEADS ONTO WIRE THAT IS TWISTED TO HOLD THE BEADS IN PLACE. MAKING BEADED FLOWER-AND-FOLIAGE CORSAGES, TIARAS AND BROOCHES WAS A POPULAR VICTORIAN PASTIME. MIX A FEW SMALL COLORED BEADS AND USE TRANSLUCENT ONES INSTEAD OF OPAQUE TO MIMIC THE DELICATE HUES FOUND IN NATURAL PETALS AND LEAVES.

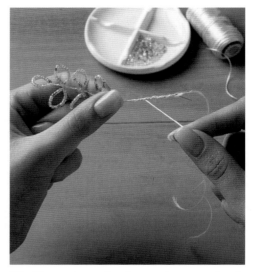

1 To make the leaves, cut 8¾ inches of 0.4 mm wire. Twist a small knot in one end to prevent the beads from falling off. Mix a few pink beads with the yellow. Bend the wire in half, thread on 18 beads, push up to the bend, then twist the wire together to form a beaded loop.

2 Wind the working wire around and down the stem ¼ inch, make another loop and thread on 18 more beads. Wrap the working wire around the stem another time and make another loop at the same level. Make two more pairs of loops along the length of the stem. Twist the wire around the stem.

3 Cover the twisted stem by wrapping it with embroidery floss.

MATERIALS AND EQUIPMENT YOU WILL NEED
WIRE CUTTERS • 0.4 MM BEADING WIRE • ROUND-NOSED JEWELRY PLIERS • SMALL WHITE, PINK, YELLOW GLASS BEADS • EMBROIDERY FLOSS •
DRILL AND SMALL DRILL BIT • WOODEN FRAME • PROTECTIVE GOGGLES • 0.2 MM BEADING WIRE

4 Cut 16 inches wire to make a small flower, 20 inches for large. Bend wire 4 inches from one end, and make a small circle. Twist to form frame. Pick up a few pink beads with the white; thread 24 for small flower, 30 for a large.

6 Thread on beads, then twist the wire around the top of the loop. Thread on 16 beads to make a small flower and 24 for a large flower.

8 To make the center, thread on 12 yellow beads and twist a half spiral. Push the working wire through the center and twist it around the stem.

5 Make a loop by twisting the working wire around the circle.

7 Add more beads and twist the wire around the spiral frame. To make more petals, make four more loops positioned around the spiral frame.

9 Position bead flowers and leaves, mark these points and drill holes.

▶

10 Push the wire stems of the beaded flowers and leaves through the holes and twist them into a knot on the wrong side of the frame.

11 Trim the wire. Using the thinner wire, secure the knots on the wrong side of the frame.

BEAD CURTAIN

THIS EXOTIC WINDOW DECORATION IS DESIGNED TO MAKE THE MOST OF THE BEAUTIFUL INDIAN LAMPWORK BEADS USED. THE LIGHT FILTERING THROUGH THE CURTAIN INTENSIFIES THEIR COLOR AND INTRICATE FILIGREE WORK. ALL THE BEADS ARE GLASS, WHICH MAKES THE CURTAIN VERY HEAVY, SO IT IS IMPORTANT TO MAKE EXTRA FINAL STITCHES. THE CURTAIN DOES NOT HAVE TO COVER THE WHOLE WINDOW; THREE-QUARTER LENGTH WOULD LOOK VERY EFFECTIVE. YOU CAN ALSO MAKE A CURTAIN FOR A DOORWAY, USING PLASTIC BEADS INSTEAD OF GLASS FOR SAFETY.

1 Measure the desired width of the curtain and cut the wood to fit. Mark points 1 inch apart and 1 inch from the edge, as shown. Drill holes at these points.

2 For every hole, cut a length of fishing twine to double the desired length of the curtain plus 24 inches. Thread both ends through the hole, then through the loop, and pull taut. Try to keep the loops untangled.

3 Working from left to right, thread on the following beads: (length 1) eight blue and one lampwork, (length 2) 12 blue and one lampwork, (length 3) 16 blue and one lampwork, (length 4) 12 blue and one lampwork. Repeat sequence to complete the width of the curtain.

4 For row 2, again working from left to right, add 16 blue beads and one lampwork bead. For row 3, add 12 blue and one lampwork. For row 4, add eight blue beads and one lampwork bead.

5 For row 5, add four blue, one green, two blue, one green, one blue, one green, one blue, 12 green, a lampwork.

6 For row 6, add 20 green and a lampwork. On alternate strands, add three green and a pendant. Pass all strands back through the last beads. Finish with a knot below the last lampwork. Knot each strand up through itself, and make seven more knots. On alternate strands, add a green bead. Pass strand back up through penultimate bead. Make several finishing knots.

MATERIALS AND EQUIPMENT YOU WILL NEED

TAPE MEASURE • SAW • WOODEN PICTURE RAIL, AT LEAST TWO INCHES WIDE • PENCIL • DRILL AND FINE DRILL BIT • FISHING TWINE • SCISSORS • ¼-INCH BLUE OVAL GLASS BEADS • LAMPWORK BEADS • ¼-INCH GREEN OVAL GLASS BEADS • LARGE GLASS PENDANTS

WATERFALL SCREEN

SHIMMERING DROPLETS OF WATER APPEAR TO CASCADE DOWN THIS STUNNING MODERN SCREEN. THE EFFECT IS CREATED BY TRANSPARENT PLASTIC CRYSTALS SUSPENDED ON FINE SILVER EMBROIDERY THREAD. USE BEADS OF DIFFERENT SIZES TO GIVE INTEREST TO THE DESIGN. THE MACHINE EMBROIDERY THREAD CAN BE USED DIRECTLY FROM THE REEL WITHOUT THE NEED FOR A BEADING NEEDLE OF ANY KIND. MAKE THREE MATCHING PANELS FOR A FREESTANDING SCREEN.

1 For each panel, cut two pieces of wood 55 inches long and two pieces 16 inches long. Sand thoroughly.

2 Place the two short pieces across either end of the long pieces. Position the brackets on the inside of each corner and mark the position of the screws. Using a drill bit to match, make holes at these points. Screw the brackets in place.

3 Paint the panel with two coats of white latex paint and let dry. Paint the spheres with two coats of silver paint and let dry.

MATERIALS AND EQUIPMENT YOU WILL NEED

SAW • 12 YARDS 2 x 2-INCH WOOD • SANDPAPER AND SANDING BLOCK • 12 RIGHT-ANGLED BRACKETS AND SCREWS •
DRILL AND DRILL BITS • SCREWDRIVER • PAINTBRUSH • WHITE LATEX PAINT • 12 WOOD SPHERES, 2¼ INCHES IN DIAMETER •
SILVER PAINT • HAMMER • LONG NAILS • ½-INCH-DIAMETER PLASTIC TUBING • 6 HINGES • 12 SCREWS • DOWELLING • TRANSPARENT
PLASTIC CRYSTAL BEADS, IN VARIOUS SIZES • TWO REELS SILVER MACHINE EMBROIDERY THREAD • SMALL SILVER GLASS BEADS • SCISSORS

4 Hammer in a nail 1¼ inches from the top and bottom on the inside edge of each side strut.

5 For each panel, cut two pieces of plastic tubing 18 inches long and push over the protruding nails.

6 Mark the position of the hinges on the side edges of the panels, 12 inches from top and bottom. Check that the screen will fold, then screw in place.

7 Mark the position of the spheres at the four corners. Cut four pieces of dowelling 2 inches long. Drill holes in the frame and the spheres with a drill bit the size of the dowelling. Push dowelling into the spheres, then into the frame.

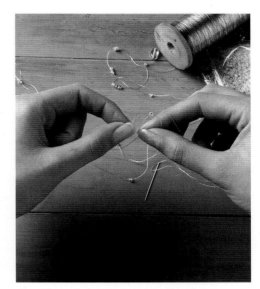

8 Thread the transparent beads in random sequence directly onto one of the reels of silver thread. Leave 4–12-inch gaps between groups of beads, knotting thread after each group.

9 Thread on a plastic bead, then pass the thread through the bead again. Thread on small silver glass beads in groups of three or more. Fasten off the end of the thread and cut.

▶

10 Unravel a little thread from the other silver reel. Tie one end to the lower piece of tubing on the first panel. Pass the reel over the tubing at the top, then under the lower tubing. Continue back and forth across the width of the panel.

11 Wrap the beaded thread around the tubing in the same way. Repeat with the other panels.

FRINGED LAMPSHADE

GLASS BEADS ARE AT THEIR MOST BEAUTIFUL AND MAGICAL WHEN LIT FROM BEHIND. EVEN A PLAIN PAPER SHADE CAN BE TRANSFORMED WITH A LONG BEAD FRINGE. THE SEQUENCE OF BEAD COLORS VARIES SLIGHTLY, TO TIE IN WITH THE HAND-PAINTED STRIPES AND ADD EXTRA INTEREST. IT IS IMPORTANT TO USE A GRAPH-PAPER GUIDE SO THAT YOU CAN CHECK THAT EACH STRAND OF BEADS IS THE SAME LENGTH.

1 Draw freehand stripes of varying widths down the length of the lamp-shade. Let dry.

2 Using a sharp needle, pierce a row of holes ¼ inch apart just above the bottom rim.

3 Cut yellow thread twice the desired length of the fringe plus 10 inches and double through the beading needle. Pass the needle through a hole on a yellow stripe, then loop through and pull taut.

4 Mark bead sequence on graph paper. Thread on small beads: 4½ inches of yellow, one purple, one yellow, one purple and one yellow. Add a bugle, then alternate five small yellow and four purple. (On alternate strands, add an extra two of each color.) Add three yellow.

5 Add one purple teardrop and three yellow beads. Insert the needle just below the purple teardrop and make a final stitch, checking that no thread is showing. Pass the needle up the strand.

6 Make a stitch below the bugle, then pass the needle and thread up through the bugle, and make another stitch. Pull gently on the strand to remove kinks. Continue around the shade. For the white stripes, use white thread and substitute transparent beads for yellow ones.

MATERIALS AND EQUIPMENT YOU WILL NEED
YELLOW OIL-BASED MARKER • TUBULAR WHITE PAPER LAMPSHADE • TAPE MEASURE • SHARP SEWING NEEDLE • SCISSORS •
YELLOW AND WHITE BEADING THREAD • BEADING NEEDLE • PENCIL • GRAPH PAPER • SMALL YELLOW GLASS BEADS • SMALL PURPLE GLASS BEADS •
1¼-INCH PURPLE BUGLE BEADS • PURPLE TEARDROP BEADS • SMALL TRANSPARENT GLASS BEADS

BEADED TASSELS

THESE BRIGHT-COLORED TASSELS ARE INSPIRED BY ETHNIC BEADWORK. STITCHED TO EITHER END OF A BOLSTER OR TO A CUSHION, THEY WOULD CERTAINLY ADD A NOTE OF DRAMA TO AN INTERIOR DESIGN SCHEME. FOR A MORE ELEGANT LOOK, USE TRANSLUCENT OR METALLIC BEADS. THE FIRST TWO TASSELS HAVE TRADITIONAL WRAPPED "HEADS"; THE THIRD USES A LARGE BEAD AS THE "HEAD". CHECK EACH STRAND AGAINST A GRAPH-PAPER GUIDE AS YOU WORK.

1 For the turquoise and red tassel: Cut a piece of tape 10 inches long. Mark the desired color sequence and the length of the tassel on graph paper. Thread the beading needle and fasten on at one end of the tape. Repeat the following sequence all along the tassel: Thread on 18 small turquoise beads, eight red beads, then one large and one small turquoise bead.

2 Using the last bead as an anchor, pass the needle up through the second-to-last bead, then all the way up the strand. Insert the needle into the tape and make a stitch to one side. Repeat along the length of the tape.

3 Roll up the tape and secure the tassel with several stitches.

MATERIALS AND EQUIPMENT YOU WILL NEED

SCISSORS • FABRIC TAPE • PENCIL • GRAPH PAPER • BEADING NEEDLE • BEADING THREAD • SMALL TURQUOISE AND RED GLASS BEADS • LARGE TURQUOISE GLASS BEADS • SEWING NEEDLE AND THREAD • TURQUOISE EMBROIDERY THREAD • MEDIUM RED CRYSTAL BEAD • SMALL WHITE AND LIGHT GREEN GLASS BEADS • TWO LARGE ORANGE GLASS BEADS • SMALL DARK GREEN GLASS BEADS • TWO MEDIUM-SIZE LIGHT GREEN GLASS BEADS

4 Fasten with embroidery thread and wrap tightly around the "head" of the tassel. Fasten securely.

6 For the looped green and white tassel: Plan an even sequence of colors on graph paper. Cut a 10-inch piece of tape and fasten with beading thread, as in step 1. Thread on the following beads: 13 white, seven green, 24 white, seven green, 13 white.

7 Insert the needle back into the tape at the same point to make a loop. Make a stitch to secure, then make a stitch to one side. Repeat along the length of the tape. ▶

5 Fasten with a beading needle and thread at the top of the bead "skirt." Thread 15 small turquoise beads to cover the curve of the "head." Insert the needle into the top and bring it out at the bottom. Pass the needle through the last bead threaded, thread on two fewer, then take over curve and through last bead at top. Insert needle from top to bottom, and repeat sequence to cover "head." At the top, pass the needle through the "head" and 20 small turquoise beads, then back through "head" to make a loop. Secure.

Below: Beaded tassels can be used in jewelry or interior design for instant added detail.

8 Complete the "head" of the tassel as in steps 3–5, adding a red crystal bead at the base of the loop.

10 Cut a length of thread, double it and thread the ends onto the needle. Fold the beaded strands in half and tie the thread loop around all the strands at this point. Pass the thread ends through the large orange bead. Thread on one medium light green crystal, 17 small light green beads, one medium light green bead and 17 small light green, then pass the needle back through the orange bead to make a loop. Secure.

9 For the green and orange tassel: Mark the desired length of the tassel strands on graph paper. Cut thread double this length and thread on four small light green beads. Using the last bead as an anchor, pass the needle through the first three beads to fasten. Thread on small beads: 20 light green, 40 dark green and 24 light green, adjusting the numbers to fill the strand. Using the last bead as an anchor, pass the needle through the second to last bead, then through the entire strand, making finishing stitches all the way along. Make eight more strands in the same way.

TEMPLATES

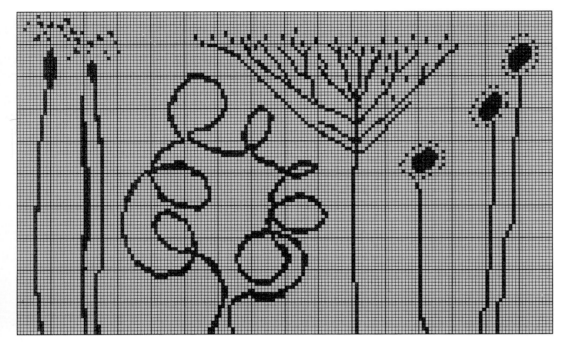

NEEDLEPOINT PHOTOGRAPH ALBUM

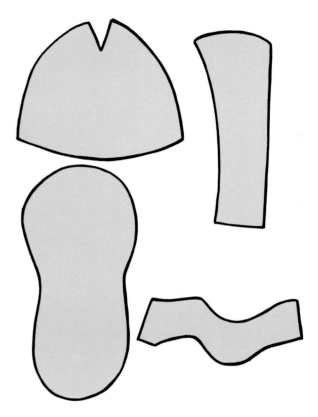

CHILD'S SLIPPERS

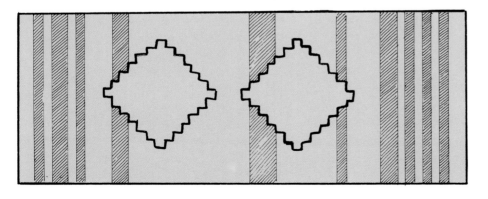

WOVEN BRACELET

PEARL TIARA

SUPPLIERS

Discount Bead House
P.O. Box 186
The Plains, OH 45780
Tel: (800) 793-7592

Ornamental Resources, Inc.
P.O. Box 3010
Idaho Springs, CO 80452
Tel: (303) 567-4988

Promenade's
P.O. Box 2092
Boulder, CO 80306
Tel: (303) 440-4807

Shipwreck Beads
5021 Mud Bay Rd.
Olympia, WA 98502
Tel: (800) 950-4232

The Garden of Beadin'
P.O. Box 1535
Redway, CA 95560
Tel: (707) 923-9120

Westcroft Beadworks
139 Washington St.
South Norwalk, CT 06854
Tel: (203) 852-9194

ACKNOWLEDGMENTS

AUTHOR'S ACKNOWLEDGMENTS
I would like to thank the contributors for their beautiful projects: Victoria Brown, Pearl Tiara;
Judy Clayton, Wrapped Earrings and Wallet; Lucinda Ganderton, Venetian Necklace, Drawstring Bag and
Creamer Cover; Daniella Zimmerman, Dramatic Painted Gloves, Velvet Bolster Cushion, Spiraled "Chandelier"
and Waterfall Screen.

Thanks are also due to Peter Williams for his patience and excellence.

PICTURE CREDITS
The publishers would like to thank the following for permission to reproduce pictures in this book: Christies' Images: p. 8,
Native American beaded cloth sash, p. 9, gloves of white kid embroidered in silver thread and sequins; The Embroiderers' Guild: p. 10,
Victorian Berlinwork vests, photographer Julia Hedgecoe, p. 11, charts, samplers and slipper tops in Berlinwork, photographer J. Hedgecoe;
the printed silk voile dress on p. 11 is reproduced courtesy of the Trustees of the Victoria and Albert Museum.

INDEX

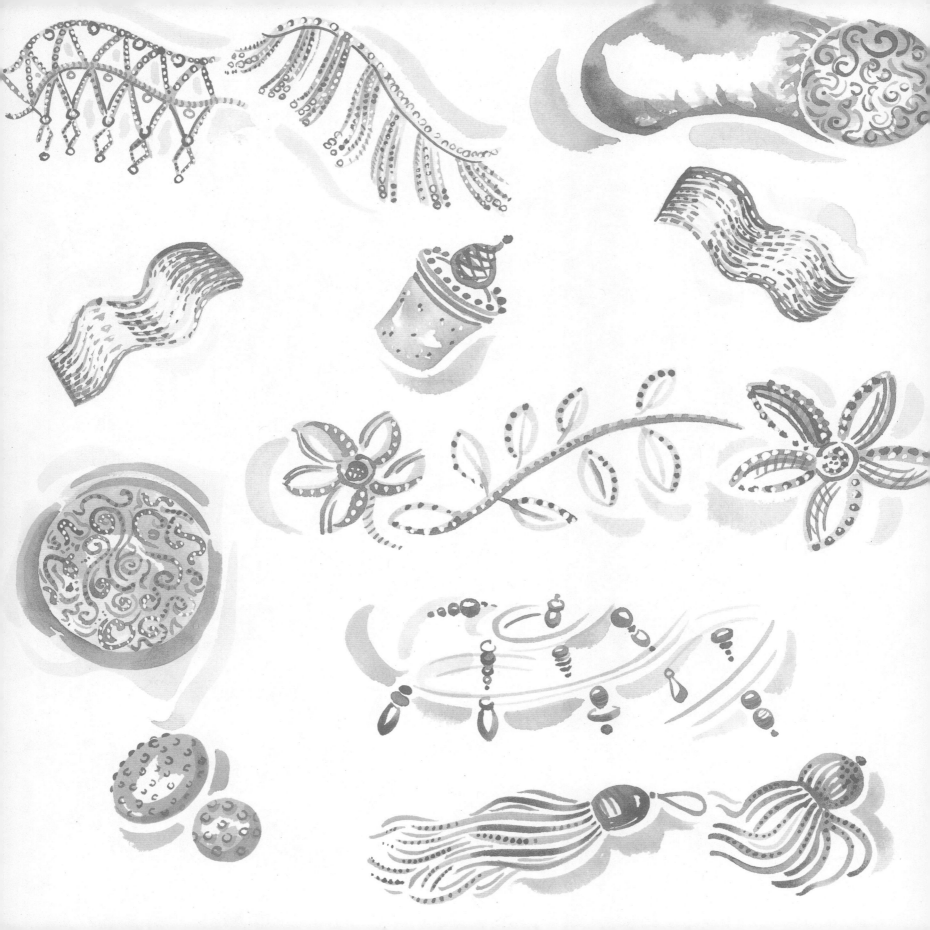